"*Star Trek and Faith* is a model of winsome engagement, identifying important theological questions raised across the *Trek* canon and showing how the Christian faith offers reasonable and even compelling answers to those questions. Whether you're a Trekkie Christian trying to reconcile your fandom with your faith, or a skeptical fan who embraces *Trek's* secular humanism, this highly accessible book is worthy of your attention—definitely recommended!"

—Matthew Carey Jordan
Vice President of Academic Affairs, Saint Mary Seminary
and Graduate School of Theology

"I confess that I am not a Trekkie, but this book made me want to become one. I love imagined universes that intersect in profound and complex ways with perennial, deeply human questions, and Mark Hansard shows, in nuanced but accessible ways, how these intersections pervade *Star Trek* in all its manifestations. Highly recommend!"

—Tim Pickavance
Professor of Philosophy, Talbot School of Theology, Biola University

"This book is an exciting and engaging dive into the spiritual and theological dimensions of *Star Trek*. Mark Hansard has done a wonderful job of digging below the surface of individual episodes to reveal their deeper meanings and Christian themes. I highly recommend it for 'Trekkies' and theology buffs alike!"

—Aaron M. Griffith
Associate Professor of Philosophy, William and Mary

"Golly, Jim. I'm a doctor, not a literary critic. Oh wait—I'm not even a doctor. But I am a longtime fan of *Star Trek*, as is Mark Hansard. Fans have long observed spiritual themes in *Star Trek*, as in any storytelling that addresses large and profound ideas. Mark discusses selected episodes of *Star Trek* vis-à-vis classic Christian doctrines, including insights from Gene Roddenberry's own point of view. The book is organized in a format that lends itself to small group study. Read. Watch. Discuss."

—Carol Regehr
Instructor Emerita, Physics Department, Kansas State University

"Mark Hansard has an excellent grasp of both *Star Trek* and apologetics and is uniquely skilled at putting the two into conversation. I'm certain that both volumes of *Star Trek and Faith* will fuel the warp engines of those seeking an engaging and nerdy way to further their ongoing voyage of faith. I, for one, am glad to have a colleague like Mark along for the journey."

—**Kevin C. Neece**
Author of *The Gospel According to Star Trek: The Original Crew*

Star Trek and Faith

—Volume 1—

Star Trek and Faith

Christian Worldview and Trek Series *New* and *Old*

—Volume 1—

MARK S. HANSARD

Foreword by Michael W. Austin

WIPF & STOCK · Eugene, Oregon

STAR TREK AND FAITH, VOLUME 1
Christian Worldview and Trek Series *New* and *Old*

Copyright © 2025 Mark S. Hansard. All rights reserved. Except for brief quotations in critical publications or reviews, no part of this book may be reproduced in any manner without prior written permission from the publisher. Write: Permissions, Wipf and Stock Publishers, 199 W. 8th Ave., Suite 3, Eugene, OR 97401.

Wipf & Stock
An Imprint of Wipf and Stock Publishers
199 W. 8th Ave., Suite 3
Eugene, OR 97401

www.wipfandstock.com

PAPERBACK ISBN: 979-8-3852-3519-3
HARDCOVER ISBN: 979-8-3852-3520-9
EBOOK ISBN: 979-8-3852-3521-6

VERSION NUMBER 072325

Unless otherwise noted, all Scripture quotations are from the *Holy Bible, New International Version*® Copyright © 1973, 1978, 1984, 2011 by Biblica, Inc.™

For my Father

Bob Hansard

1941–2025

Who first helped me with my questions about the faith.

"The steps of a good man are ordered by the Lord,
and He delights in his way."
Psalm 37:23

Contents

Foreword by Michael W. Austin | ix
Acknowledgments | xi
Star Trek *Abbreviations and Characters* | xiii
Scripture Abbreviations | xiv

SECTION I: *Star Trek*, Christianity, and Gene Roddenberry | 1

1 High Tech, Aliens, and God: *Star Trek* in the Twenty-First Century | 3
   Secular and Christian themes in Trek. *What is a worldview? The Bible's use of logic.*

2 Gene Roddenberry: A Humanist Life | 16
   Roddenberry and Secular Humanism. Why did Roddenberry put Christian themes into Trek?

SECTION II: Humanism in *Trek* | 25

Introduction | 25

3 When the Quarry Questions: "The Brightest Star" (*Discovery*) | 27
   Is Christianity manipulative? Is God a cosmic policeman? Is it wrong to doubt your faith?

4 Dark Ages or Enlightenment? "Who Watches the Watchers" (*The Next Generation*) | 37
   What is virtue theory in Ethics? Does advanced technology appear divine to primitive cultures? Is Christianity superstitious? The Prime Directive. Science and Christianity in the Middle Ages.

5 Petty Gods and Noble Humanity: "Who Mourns for Adonais?" (*The Original Series*) | 52
   Is God capricious, self-centered, and insecure? What about his wrath? God's holiness and his jealousy.

CONTENTS

SECTION III: Christianity in *Trek* | 65

Introduction | 65

**6 Free Will or Fate? "Children of the Comet"
(*Strange New Worlds*) | 67**
The doctrine of election. How do predestination and free will go together? Why would God create people if he knew they would ultimately reject him?

7 Is Faith Always Blind? "New Eden" (*Discovery*) | 76
What is Omnism? Kierkegaard and the "leap of faith." How do faith and reason go together?

**8 The Son Rises on Rome: "Bread and Circuses"
(*The Original Series*) | 87**
Christianity and pacifism. What is just war theory? Is self-defense justifiable? Morality and the use of nuclear weapons.

SECTION IV: Messianic Themes in *Trek* | 101

Introduction | 101

9 Priceless Gem: "The Empath" (*The Original Series*) | 103
What is the concept of a Messiah? Healing, love, and self-sacrifice in Isaiah 53. What is atonement and how does it relate to us?

**10 Resurrection and Rebirth: *Star Trek II* and *Star Trek III* Films
(*The Original Series*) | 113**
Spock as a messianic figure. Spock's nature and the incarnation. Jesus' life as a ransom for many. Is it rational to believe in Jesus' Resurrection?

SECTION V: Paradise in *Trek* | 127

Introduction: "Et in Arcadia Ego Part 2" (*Picard*) | 127

**11 Heaven: An Illusory Happiness? *Star Trek Generations* Film
(*Original Series* and *Next Generation*) | 129**
What is heaven like? Are there challenges in heaven? Will we be bored in heaven?

**12 Religion as the Opiate of the Masses? "Return of the Archons"
(*The Original Series*) | 144**
What is true freedom? Spiritual freedom is a paradox. Christian hedonism and the Holy Spirit. Is imperfection essential to being human?

Bibliography | 155
Index of Episodes & Films | 163
Scripture Index | 165

Foreword

GROWING UP IN THE late 1970s and early 1980s, I loved watching *Star Trek: The Original Series*. As I reflect back on why I loved this series so much, and continue to love it today, many things come to mind. I enjoyed science fiction and read a lot of it back then. So a science fiction show that had heroic yet human characters, a compelling adventure, and ultimately offered a hopeful vision for humanity and the universe was easy for me to love. Plus, the special effects were, for their time, so cool. I wanted a communicator and a phaser! I enjoyed the original *Star Trek* so much that when our family bought a VCR (video cassette recorder, for those of you who came after Generation X!), I began recording every episode I could on VHS tapes. Those tapes have long disappeared, but my love for *Star Trek* remains.

There were other science fiction shows that I watched and enjoyed, but they didn't have the same staying power for me. Why is that? Certainly I love the hopeful optimism that runs through much of *Star Trek*. But as a philosopher, I also love the way that *Star Trek* deals with so many of life's big questions, the kinds of questions most, if not all, of us think about at least from time to time. Is there a God? What is true freedom? Can faith and doubt coexist? When, if ever, is war justified? What is the best life for human beings? Should one always follow the Prime Directive? Okay, that last one is only asked by Trekkies. Whether or not you agree with the answers that the characters embrace, *Star Trek* is a wonderful example of the ways that entertainment can be deep, the ways it can lead us to question, to explore strange new worlds of ideas, and consider those ideas for ourselves.

While the characters and the special effects of other *Star Trek* series are different, the other shows in the *Star Trek* universe address these same questions, in very human ways. In recent years I've thoroughly enjoyed *Star Trek: Discovery* and *Strange New Worlds*. When I was devotedly recording *Original Series* episodes on my parents' VCR, I of course had no idea that a

Foreword

few decades later I would be able to watch both it and many other *Star Trek* series and films on demand. *Star Trek* fans can watch Kirk, Spock, McCoy, Uhura and others explore the universe, fight Romulans and Klingons, and develop deep friendships along the way any time we want. We can also watch Picard, Riker, Troi, and friends explore the galaxy in *The Next Generation*, join Christopher Pike as he discovers *Strange New Worlds*, or travel across space and time with Michael Burnham in *Discovery*. It's a great time to be a Trekkie!

Something similar is true about Mark Hansard's *Star Trek and Faith: Christian Worldview and Trek Series New and Old*. He takes the reader on a journey of asking the big questions of life with Pike, Kirk, Picard, Janeway, Sisko, Burnham, Spock, Saru, and others as our companions. But there are others who he invites us to journey with as well, expanding our list of companions exploring the universe's big questions. Ancient thinkers like the Apostle Paul, Augustine, Aquinas, and Aristotle are here, as are contemporary ones like Alvin Plantinga, Richard Swinburne, and William Lane Craig, among many others. The universe of ideas is as full of adventure, intrigue, danger, joy, and the hopes and fears of humanity as the *Star Trek* universe. Many have gone before us and have left important markers for us as we seek answers to life's perennial questions. Ideally, we reflect upon these questions not just to increase what we know, but to guide how we live. Maybe you've gone over many of these questions before. Maybe not. Either way, there is a vast territory of knowledge and wisdom available to us, and *Star Trek* is a wonderful way into this universe.

I'm grateful Mark Hansard wrote this book, and he is an excellent person to take us on this journey. He has a graduate degree in philosophy, has formal training in theology, and he's been a campus minister for 32 years. His on-the-ground experience discussing big ideas with faculty and students enables him to communicate in ways that are clear and relevant, in the best sense of those terms. He's also been a *Star Trek* fan for 46 years!

If you are interested in reflecting on some of life's big religious and philosophical questions, then read and think about the ideas in this book. Or, as Captain Picard would say, "Engage!" The universe of ideas is waiting.

Michael W. Austin
Author of *Humility: Rediscovering the Way of Love and Life in Christ*

Acknowledgments

I AM INDEBTED TO many wonderful people who stood behind me and helped make this book a reality. I am grateful to Steven Kates and Marc Cushman for their belief in the book and their invaluable support. To Mark Alfred, my editor, for his many hours of toil on the manuscript. To Matt Wimer, Emily Callihan, and the team at Wipf & Stock, for their commitment to see this book completed. To my precious wife Leanne, for her many hours of repeatedly reading and correcting the same chapters of the book. To my daughters Savannah, Annabelle, and Emily, for their input on the book and help with chapter titles. And to these people who read all or portions of the manuscript and gave their input: Michael Austin, Chris Legg, Mark Legg, Bobby Slaughter, Bob Hansard, Carrie Hansen, Mark Bernier, Garry DeWeese, Jonathan Feng, Brent Watson, Chris Gadsden, Jeff Bridgforth, Dan Flippo, Sandie Anderson, and Ron Schum. Any mistakes are, of course, my own.

Star Trek Abbreviations and Characters

TOS—*Star Trek: The Original Series* (1966–1969) Characters: Capt. Kirk, Mr. Spock, Dr. McCoy, Scotty, Lt. Uhura, Lt. Sulu, and Ensign Chekov. Includes the first six *Star Trek* films.

TAS—*Star Trek: The Animated Series* (1973–1974) This show has the same crew as *The Original Series*, minus Chekov.

TNG—*Star Trek: The Next Generation* (1987–1994) Characters: Capt. Picard, Cmdr. (Commander) Riker, Cmdr. Data (an android), Counselor Troi, Lt. Worf, Dr. Crusher, Cmdr. La Forge (a blind crewman whose visor allows him to see), Guinan.

DIS—*Star Trek: Discovery* (2017–2024) Characters: Admiral Burnham, Ambassador Saru, Lt. Tilly, Dr. Culber, Cmdr. Stamets, Philippa Georgiou, Capt. Pike, Ash Tyler, 'Book" Booker, President T'Rina.

PIC—*Star Trek: Picard* (2020–2023) Characters: Admiral Picard (retired), Dr. Jurati, Soji Asha (an android), Elnor, Raffi, Chris Rios, Narek, Seven of Nine, Geordi La Forge, William Riker, Deanna Troi, Worf, Data, Beverly Crusher, Jack Crusher.

SNW—*Star Trek: Strange New Worlds* (2022–) Characters: Captain Pike, Mr. Spock, Number One (Una), Cadet Uhura, Nurse Chapel, Lt. Noonien-Singh.

Scripture Abbreviations

OT—Old Testament
Gen—Genesis
Exod—Exodus
Lev—Leviticus
Deut—Deuteronomy
1 Sam—1 Samuel
2 Sam—2 Samuel
1 Kgs—1 Kings
1 Chr—1 Chronicles
2 Chr—2 Chronicles
Ps/Pss—Psalm/Psalms
Prov—Proverbs
Hos—Hosea
Song—Song of Songs
Isa—Isaiah
Jer—Jeremiah
Lam—Lamentations
Ezek—Ezekiel
Dan—Daniel
Zeph—Zephaniah

NT—New Testament
Matt—Matthew
Rom—Romans
1 Cor—1 Corinthians
2 Cor—2 Corinthians
Gal—Galatians
Eph—Ephesians
Phil—Philippians
2 Tim—2 Timothy
Heb—Hebrews
Jas—James
2 Pet—2 Peter
Rev—Revelation

SECTION I

Star Trek, Christianity, and Gene Roddenberry

1

High Tech, Aliens, and God

Star Trek in the Twenty-First Century

Number One, Captain Pike, and Mr. Spock from *Star Trek: Strange New Worlds*. Promotional image: CBS Studios and Paramount Pictures Corp.

FROM STAR TREK: STRANGE *New Worlds* to *The Original Series* of the 1960s, *Star Trek* has always explored deep religious and philosophical questions. Is there a God? If he exists, how would that change our knowledge of ourselves and our place in the universe? What is human nature, and how ought humans to flourish? What is the meaning of life?

SECTION I: *STAR TREK*, CHRISTIANITY, AND GENE RODDENBERRY

Older iterations of *Trek* famously explored these ideas, but exciting new *Trek* series carry on the tradition. Today we live in a golden age of the *Star Trek* Universe, with multiple series available for streaming on Paramount+. After *Star Trek: Discovery*'s successful premiere in 2017, Paramount launched *Star Trek: Picard* in 2020 and *ST: Strange New Worlds* in 2022. Two animated series premiered as well: *Star Trek: Lower Decks* and *Star Trek: Prodigy*. While *Discovery*, *Picard*, and *Lower Decks* have ended, more *Trek* series are in production. As of this writing, eleven series and thirteen films have been produced over the history of the franchise, and *Star Trek* shows no signs of slowing down.

As we will see, philosophical and religious ideas in these new streaming series harken back to religious themes in earlier *Trek* episodes. In the *Discovery* episode "New Eden," for example, the advanced technology of the *Discovery* crew is mistaken for divine power. Captain Pike quotes a variation of Arthur C. Clarke's third law: "Any sufficiently advanced extraterrestrial intelligence is indistinguishable from God." Such themes trace their roots back to older *Trek* episodes like "Who Mourns for Adonais?" (TOS) and "Who Watches the Watchers" (TNG).

Significantly, in all of these episodes, it *looked* as if God (or other divine beings) were there, but they weren't really there at all. Either aliens were mistaken for gods, or high-tech gadgetry was mistaken for supernatural power.

There are Christian themes in *Star Trek* as well, and Christian imagery in *Strange New Worlds* harkens back to earlier Christian themes in *The Original Series*. In the SNW episode "All Those Who Wander" (see volume 2), Lieutenant Hemmer realizes he is a carrier of alien embryos that will inevitably attack and kill the crew. He sacrifices his life "to save the lives of those I most care about," echoing Spock's decision in *Star Trek II* to sacrifice his life because "the needs of the many outweigh the needs of the few." Both Spock and Hemmer are messianic figures who echo Jesus' decision to give his life "as a ransom for many."

Star Trek has been exploring such philosophical and religious ideas for decades and entertaining us along the way. The answers *Trek* provides to questions about God's existence and what that means for human flourishing are essential because *Star Trek* continues to have a tremendous cultural impact today. *Trek* episodes, both new and old, are viewed thousands of times annually worldwide. With a global reach of this scale, how does *Star*

Trek influence the way we think about God, ourselves, and our place in the universe?

THE IMPACT OF ENTERTAINMENT MEDIA

Today more than ever, entertainment outlets, news channels, and social media shape the way people think. From pop lyrics to political arguments to internet conspiracy theories, we are bombarded with messages every day. Not surprisingly, studies show they influence us. For example, researchers have found that watching certain news channels influences how people vote. In one landmark study, educational children's programming *raised* the IQ of children who watched it by five points.[1] Even fiction can have a powerful effect. When *Black Panther* premiered in 2018, the motto "*Black Panther* is more than a movie—it's a movement" caught fire. The Electoral Justice Project even used characters from *Black Panther* to encourage people to vote.[2] Such media can have positive social effects if they have high quality or educational content, and neutral to negative effects if they have low quality or purely entertainment content.[3]

When it comes to negative media influence, can certain programming pull Christian viewers away from their values? What if watching a show like *Star Trek* can create doubts about their faith? It did for me.

When I was ten years old, I saw *Star Trek: The Motion Picture* for the first time. I was captivated by the technology, the music, and the profoundly thoughtful ending. A machine that could come alive and ask questions about the meaning of life? I had to see more. I began watching reruns of *The Original Series* evenings during dinner at my home.

But as I absorbed the *Star Trek* universe, Clarke's third law took hold, and I began to doubt my Christian faith. Was Jesus merely an extraterrestrial, visiting Earth with superior technology that made it *appear* that he was doing miracles? Was the story of his resurrection simply a myth like the Greek myths of old? These questions gnawed at me for quite some time, until finally I had the courage to ask my father about them. He graciously replied that these were excellent questions, and that Christian thinkers and writers had already thought about them. He gave me a book from his

---

1. See Rothwell, "You Are What You Watch?," paras. 7–12.

2. See Jenkins, "Black Panther," paras. 1–2; and Lockhart, "#WakandaTheVote," paras. 1–5.

3. Rothwell, "You Are What You Watch?," paras. 3–4, 13–21.

shelf that defended the Christian faith with reason and evidence, a strategy known as Christian apologetics.[4] I came to believe that it was rational to believe Jesus was real and that he did in fact rise from the dead.

Why did *Star Trek* cause me to doubt my faith? Because every time a divine figure appeared in the original show, it was either a supercomputer gone awry or an arrogant alien masquerading as a god. Nothing that appeared divine actually turned out to be divine, and there were no regular characters in the show who had any religious beliefs at all. The secular humanism in *Trek* had influenced my thinking and thus my worldview. But when I started reading defenses of Christianity, I realized that *Star Trek* wasn't telling me the truth about God. It was simply telling me one perspective, a skeptical perspective.

Thus, all kinds of media, both fiction and nonfiction, can influence us. Hollywood films have also harnessed the power of filmmaking to plant ideas into viewers' minds. For example, the 2010 movie *Inception* by director Christopher Nolan traded on the double meaning of "inception." The protagonists in the film tried to plant an idea into a man's mind using his dreams, in the same way that a movie director plants ideas into the minds of an audience. Just as in the film, a moviegoer is unaware that an idea is being planted because the ideas in a movie can be placed between especially emotive scenes or flashy special effects. In other words, the ideas in the film can bypass the moviegoer's rational thought processes. If the viewer does not apply critical thinking skills to the idea, then essentially he is being at best influenced, or at worst, controlled by someone else who has a vested interest in controlling him or moving him to action.[5]

The question is, should Christians simply absorb ideas from the media, or critically analyze them? Without analyzing such ideas, followers of Christ could see their spiritual lives atrophy, or worse, disintegrate.

On the other hand, it is important to remember that many ideas in movies are good ideas, are consistent with a Christian worldview, and should be adopted. From series about Jesus such as *The Chosen*, to science fiction franchises such as *Star Wars* or *Ender's Game* that clearly delineate between good and evil, many themes in the media can strengthen a Christian's outlook. As well, many films have themes that are not explicitly Christian but fit with a Christian worldview, such as *Gattaca*, which warns against genetic manipulation and eugenics, and *Arrival*, which chooses

---

4. The book he gave me was Josh McDowell's *Evidence That Demands a Verdict*.
5. See Johnson, *Inception and Philosophy*, 126–28.

love over a predetermined future. Even films that offer a more subtle and complicated view of evil can be instructive.

Thus, it is necessary to think critically about entertainment media in order to see what themes fit with a Christian worldview, and what themes are antithetical to Scripture. We also need to understand that most films have themes that aren't specifically addressed in Scripture, but many of these themes are true anyway. For the Christian, it is not necessary to discard ideas that *aren't in* Scripture, only ideas that *contradict* Scripture.

STAR TREK'S CULTURAL IMPACT

When *Star Trek* debuted on NBC in 1966, few could have imagined the global impact it would have. But it soon became clear in the early 1970s that *Star Trek*, already enormously popular, was becoming a cultural phenomenon.[6] When NASA announced construction of the first Space Shuttle, Trekkies[7] organized a letter-writing campaign to the White House. Four hundred thousand letters deluged the Oval Office asking President Gerald Ford to name the shuttle *Enterprise*, after the famous starship on the show. Ford agreed. The Space Shuttle *Enterprise* was rolled out in September of 1976 as the *Star Trek* fanfare played in the background.[8] "It was spine-tingling," recalled Walter Koenig, the actor who played Ensign Chekov. "It was chilling to think that a TV show has permeated that many strata of society."[9]

Thus, *Star Trek* joined an elite club of television shows that went from popular to *iconic*. Iconic shows even influence people who have never seen an episode. For example, linguists believe that the pronunciation of the term "data" morphed into a long "A" after the character "Data" became popular on *Star Trek: The Next Generation*. And there are new phrases in English that people understand today, such as "Beam me up, Scotty," or "warp speed," even if they've never seen a *Trek* episode. *Star Trek* has influenced how we pronounce words and even how we communicate, and it continues that influence today.

---

6. For a description of the syndication ratings for TOS in the 1970s, see Alexander, *Star Trek Creator*, 447.

7. For the debate on using "Trekkie" vs. "Trekker" see Memory Alpha Wiki, "Trekkie," paras. 1–7.

8. Alexander, *Star Trek Creator*, 429–30.

9. Cushman, *Voyages: 1970s Volume 2*, 137.

Trek has also influenced the development of technology. Jeff Bezos' motivation for founding his space exploration company Blue Origin, for example, was influenced by his love of *Star Trek*. His development of Amazon's Alexa is patterned after the computer on the *Enterprise*, which talked to crew members, listened, and gave responses.[10] In fact, the History Channel produced several documentaries on *Star Trek* and technology in the early 2000s, which interviewed physicists and engineers about *Trek* technology that was emulated in the real world.[11]

Today, it is easy to see that *The Original Series* was ahead of its time. The first *Enterprise* crew was multiracial and multicultural, including an African American communications officer (Uhura), a Japanese American helmsman (Sulu), a Scottish chief engineer (Scotty), and a Russian navigator (Chekov—notable at the time because relations between the U.S. and the Soviet Union were dismal). Finally, Vulcan science officer Spock brought both alien and logical perspectives to the show.

Star Trek, in fact, had the first interracial kiss on television, between Lt. Uhura and Captain Kirk in "Plato's Stepchildren." Martin Luther King himself encouraged Nichelle Nichols, who played Lt. Uhura, to continue in her role on the show as it gave hope to black Americans across the country. According to Nichols, "[He] . . . approached me and said something along the lines of 'Nichelle, whether you like it or not, you have become a symbol. If you leave, they can replace you . . . and it will be like you were never there. What you've accomplished, for all of us, will only be real if you stay.' That got me thinking about how it would look for fans of color around the country if they saw me leave. I saw that this was bigger than just me."[12] Luckily for fans everywhere, Nichols stayed on the show. Today's new *Trek* series carry on this rich tradition.

STAR TREK AND WORLDVIEW

Given *Star Trek*'s continued cultural influence, it's essential to ask what kind of worldviews it endorses through its stories. Every television show or movie promotes a worldview of some sort. A worldview is a holistic way of looking at the world: It includes beliefs about where the universe comes

---

10. Andrews and Roberts, "Love Affair," paras. 16–17.

11. Memory Alpha Wiki, "Modern Marvels," para. 1; NASA, "Star Trek and NASA," paras. 1–3; and Loffhagen, "15 Star Trek Gadgets," paras. 4–8, 12–28.

12. See Ohlheiser, "How Martin Luther King," paras. 1–11.

from, whether there is a God, what the purpose of human beings is and how they flourish, how to distinguish right from wrong, and many other ideas. Every person has a worldview, whether they have heard the term or not. Everyone has views or assumptions about the purpose of life, where the universe came from, and so forth. In fact, if a person has *any views at all*, they are at the very least relying on an incipient worldview to fashion them.

Worldviews can be explicit or implicit. Every story, whether in a movie, a series, or a book, promotes a worldview either explicitly or implicitly. Often what is most important about a story is what it assumes: not something it explicitly describes, but what it assumes *underneath* what it describes. These things may not be immediately obvious, but they can have a tremendous impact on our thinking. For example, *Star Trek* stories often assume that whatever problem faced by the crew can be solved by science. Sometimes this assumption is brought out explicitly. For example, in a story in which a planet may be destroyed by a meteor, the technology of the *Enterprise* can determine the meteor's trajectory and divert it, saving the planet. But implicitly, many scenes assume the primacy of science. For example, every time Mr. Spock turns on his tricorder to examine something, the implication is that only science can determine what that thing is. The idea that science can save humanity and show us what's real and what to believe, is very powerful. If, as viewers, we are not aware that these ideas are being promoted, we may begin to believe that only science can tell us what is real. But what of beliefs about God, salvation, or heaven that are rational to believe through Christian theology or philosophy? Such beliefs, like a multitude of others, can indeed be rational even though they are not discovered or known through scientific investigation.

In fact, most of what we believe is not based on scientific evidence at all. The vast majority of our scientific beliefs are not based on direct knowledge or experimentation, but on the testimony of other scientists who report in their papers or textbooks the results of their experiments and how they were carried out. We don't witness the experiments or do the research ourselves. With history, too, nearly all our beliefs are based on the testimony of those who witnessed it, or the conclusions of historians who study it later. We do not witness the events themselves. Thus, most of our beliefs about the world are based on *testimony*, not on scientific investigation.

Scientism, the belief that scientific knowledge is superior to all other forms of knowledge, or it is the *only way* to have knowledge at all, is logically suspect for another reason. Scientific investigation itself must make nonscientific assumptions in order to be carried out. For example, the assumption that our minds and our senses (sight, smell, etc.) are able to understand the external world accurately is foundational to scientific investigation. But this idea is not itself scientifically provable. As well, the idea that the universe is ordered and can be rationally understood is also not scientifically provable. It is a philosophical assumption which goes back centuries to the Judeo-Christian idea that a rational God created an ordered world. Therefore, the foundations of scientific investigation are themselves philosophical, not scientific. We must rely on other ways of knowing, in addition to science, to understand the world.[13]

Returning to the idea of a worldview, while the worldview of a story can have a negative effect on one's thinking, it can also have an immensely positive impact. For example, Harriet Beecher Stowe's novel *Uncle Tom's Cabin*, published in 1852, convinced many in this country that slavery was indeed immoral and hastened the onset of the Civil War. When Stowe met President Lincoln at the White House, he is reported to have said, "So you are the little woman who wrote the book that started this great war."[14]

Entertainment media can have positive impacts as well. The original iteration of *America's Most Wanted*, a reality TV series about fugitive criminals, celebrated its one-thousandth capture in 2008 after twenty years of being on the air. And it led show host John Walsh to found the National Center for Missing and Exploited Children.[15]

Star Trek has positively influenced many other fronts, too. When *Star Trek IV*, a time-travel tale in which the *Enterprise* must save twentieth-century whales, was released in 1986, Greenpeace fielded hundreds of calls and letters asking whether whales were still being hunted as depicted in the film. Many inquiries included donations to the organization. Although Greenpeace does not know specifically how much their uptick in donations was due to the movie or how much was due to a fundraising campaign, they were grateful for the help.[16]

---

13. For a further analysis of scientism, see Craig and Moreland, *Philosophical Foundations*, 370–73.

14. It is debated whether Lincoln actually said this. See Sachsman et al., *Memory and Myth*, 8.

15. Moore, "America's Most Wanted"; and Ferguson, "Groundbreaking TV shows," para. 4.

16. See Associated Press, "Star Trek IV," paras. 1–6.

Thus, the worldview of a novel, film, or a streaming series can have a positive or a negative impact on its viewers as well as society. Some *Star Trek* stories have Christian themes that promote a Christian worldview, while some markedly undermine a Christian worldview. How can we tell the difference?

ASKING WORLDVIEW QUESTIONS

The way to determine what worldview a story promotes is to ask insightful questions about it, to discover its hidden layers and assumptions. Worldview questions ask things such as: What does the dialogue reveal about how the characters see the universe, what they assume is true, and how they ought to respond in their circumstances? What does the author or character *overlook* about what could be true of the world or how to handle a challenging situation? In other words, what does the story *assume* is real about the world?

For example, in one TNG episode, Captain Picard says, "[The Mintakans] abandoned their belief in the supernatural. Now you are asking me to sabotage that achievement, to send them back into the Dark Ages of superstition and ignorance and fear?" Here Picard is equating religious belief with crippling superstition. What does he assume about science, religion, and the Middle Ages? Is he associating religion with ignorance and fear? (We'll discuss this episode and analyze it in chapter 4.)

For another example, the TOS episode "Return of the Archons" uses religious language such as "lawgiver," "the Body," "heard the word and disobeyed," and "joy, peace, and tranquility." These phrases echo biblical language, but in the episode, they are associated with mind control. Is the "joy and peace" of which the Bible speaks only gained through God's control of our minds? Is it possible to be filled with joy and tranquility and retain our freedom? (We'll discuss this episode in chapter 12.)

Asking these questions is essential to uncovering what the story assumes about the world, how the world works, and what the right thing to do is in certain circumstances. In other words, we need to think critically about the stories we watch.

WHAT IS CRITICAL THINKING?

Critical thinking does not mean being overly critical or pessimistic. We often think of someone who is critical as being negative or perfectionistic. Critical thinking actually means using logic and reason to discover truth.[17] We need to use logic and reason to take information, evidence, and viewpoints and sift them objectively to discover whether what is being presented in a *Star Trek* story is true or partially correct. We can then create a filter to better interpret not just *Star Trek*, but any story we watch or read.

Once we analyze a story, we can take our analysis into conversations with friends. *Star Trek* is perfect for this kind of analysis because it explores philosophical, religious, and social themes using science fiction stories as a backdrop. Such themes are often assumed to be true today, and thinking about them allows us to have deeper conversations with others.

In the "Worldview Analysis" section of each chapter, you'll learn how to analyze the dialogue or plot of a certain episode to see what worldviews it promotes and compare it to a Christian worldview. In other words, you'll learn how to think critically and reap the rewards of this in your understanding of the world and of Christian ideas.

LOGIC AND THE SCRIPTURES

When we use critical thinking to analyze a story, this presupposes that logic and reason aid us in discovering the truth. But is it scriptural to rely on logic? If Christians are to lead deeply spiritual lives, isn't it unnecessary, or even detrimental to use logic?

Many followers of Christ today feel that if there is evidence to believe in Jesus, they don't have to have any faith. But this is not a biblical idea. Reason and faith go together, and biblically, the use of reason and logic is not opposed to the spiritual life. Jesus and the apostles used logic and critical thinking to interpret Scripture and to preach the gospel.

For example, Jesus used logic to clarify theology about the Messiah and dispute the Pharisees' understanding of Scripture. (The Messiah is the promised figure in the Old Testament who would come and save Israel. The Pharisees were a sect of religious leaders in Jesus' day.) In Matt 22 we have a fascinating passage:

---

17. For an introduction to critical thinking, see Lau and Chan, "Critical Thinking Web"; and Moreland, *Love Your God*.

> While the Pharisees were gathered together, Jesus asked them, "What do you think about the Messiah? Whose son is he?" "The son of David," they replied. He said to them, "How is it then that David, speaking by the Spirit, calls him 'Lord'? For he says, 'The LORD said to my Lord: "Sit at my right hand until I put your enemies under your feet.' If then David calls him 'Lord,' how can he be his son?" No one could say a word in reply, and from that day on no one dared to ask him any more questions. (Matt 22:41–46)

Here Jesus is quoting Ps 110, which was considered a psalm about the Messiah. In the psalm, David says, "The LORD said to my Lord: 'Sit at my right hand.'" But since David was king of Israel, who could be his Lord? There are two "Lords" in the passage. The first "LORD" is in all capitals because it is a translation of the Hebrew word *Yahweh*, which is God's personal name in the Old Testament. *Yahweh* (God) is clearly David's Lord. The second "Lord" refers to the Messiah. But if the Messiah was a descendent of David, why would David call him "Lord"? All of David's children would have called *him* lord, because he was their king. Here a descendent of David is David's Lord, which does not make sense unless the second "Lord" is something more than David's merely human descendent.

As Dallas Willard points out, Jesus is using a *reductio ad absurdum* argument here, which is Latin for "reduce to the absurd."[18] It takes a statement and says: If this statement is true, a second statement must also be true, but the second statement is absurd. Therefore, the first statement must also be false. Here is an example of a *reductio ad absurdum*:

1. If Jones was at the game at 3 p.m. yesterday, he was not in his house at 3 p.m. yesterday.
2. We were with Jones in his house at 3 p.m. yesterday.
3. If Jones was at the game at 3 p.m. *and* at his house at 3 p.m., he was at two places at once, which is absurd.
4. Therefore, Jones was not at the game at 3 p.m. yesterday.

Here is Jesus' *reductio ad absurdum*:

1. If the Messiah is merely the human descendent of David, David could not have called him "Lord."
2. But David did call the Messiah "Lord" in Ps 110:1.

---

18. See Willard, "Jesus the Logician," paras. 6, 23–24.

3. To believe the Messiah was David's Lord and merely his human descendent is absurd.
4. Therefore, the Messiah is not merely a human descendant of David.

Here we see that Jesus' logic runs circles around the Pharisees. He uses logic here to imply that the Messiah would be divine. And since the Scriptures are clear that Jesus was filled with the Spirit during his earthly ministry, using logic is not opposed to the spiritual life (see for example, Luke 4:1, 14, 10:21).

Since Jesus used reason to discover truth, his followers can as well. In fact, using logic is one of the main ways God has given us to discover truth. While it *is* true that many beliefs Christians hold are revealed to us by God (in Scripture or through the Holy Spirit, for example), we must use reason to understand God's revelation. In fact, to understand anything at all.

For example, to read English and understand it, one must use the rules of English grammar. Such rules include a position for the subject of a sentence, the predicate, and so forth. We must use reason to determine the order of the words, and hence their meaning. Because there is an order to the grammar, it is impossible to use grammar without reason, just as in math, where there is an order that must be understood for a problem to be solved. Thus, whenever we read or write *at all*, we are using reason, since every language has its own grammatical rules. The fact that God communicated to his people through written language means he used reason to reveal things to us.

Going back to the first centuries of Christianity, the church fathers quoted John chapter 1 to show that God is a God of reason.[19] "In the beginning was the Word, and the Word was with God, and the Word was God" (John 1:1). The Greek term for "word" here is *logos*, from which we derive our word "logic." It means "word" or "reason."

As well, Jesus tells his followers to love God with their minds: "Love the Lord your God with all your heart, all your soul, all your *mind*, and all your strength" (Mark 12:30). Here Jesus quotes Deut 6:5, which says, "Love the Lord your God with all your heart and with all your soul and with all your strength." Jesus adds the word "mind," not to emphasize the mind above all other aspects of who we are, but to explain that we must love God

---

19. For example, Tertullian, *Against Praxeas*, ch. 5–6.

with our *whole selves*, including our minds. Our minds are important to God too.

Several interesting passages in the Bible describe how God uses his people when they set their minds to study. Ezra 7:10 says, "For Ezra had devoted himself to the *study* and observance of the Law of the Lord, and to teaching its decrees and laws in Israel." Here, God uses Ezra's study of the Scriptures to help him lead the nation. And in certain passages, God blesses not only the study of Scripture or theology but other topics as well. For example, Acts 7:22 says, "Moses was educated in all the wisdom of the Egyptians and was powerful in speech and action." God used Moses' *Egyptian* training to make Moses into a great leader. We also see in Dan 1:4 and 1:17 that God used the Babylonian training that Daniel and his friends received to make them great leaders as well. Assuming that what we are learning does not contradict what God has already revealed, he can use the study of all sorts of nonreligious topics for his glory.

In the following chapters we will use critical thinking to compare the worldview of a *Trek* story with a Christian worldview. But first, we need to explore how Gene Roddenberry created *Star Trek*.

2

Gene Roddenberry
A Humanist Life

Gene Roddenberry, 1966. Courtesy Gerald Gurian.

STAR TREK IS AND continues to be the vision of one man: writer and producer Gene Roddenberry. He created *The Original Series* in 1966, the *Animated Series* in 1973, and *The Next Generation* in 1987. Although he passed away in 1991, today's *Trek* series carefully follow Roddenberry's vision of the future. We see this in interviews with Alex Kurtzman, the creator and executive producer of the various new *Trek* series streaming on Paramount+. Kurtzman consistently declares that he wants to be "very true" to Roddenberry's vision and reiterates "how important it is to see the world through Gene Roddenberry's eyes."[1]

What made Roddenberry the man that he became, and how did he see the world? What was his vision of the future?

Roddenberry was born in El Paso, Texas, in 1921, and his family moved to Los Angeles in 1923 after his father took a job as a police officer there. His father was a religious skeptic, but often allowed Gene to attend church with his mother, who was a Baptist.

Roddenberry recalled a time when, as a child, he was taken to church on communion Sunday:

> I remember complete astonishment because what they were talking about were things that were just crazy . . . You eat this wafer and you are eating the body of Christ and drinking his blood. My first impression was "This is a bunch of cannibals they put me down among!" . . . From that time it was clear to me that religion was largely nonsense, was largely magical, superstitious things.[2]

Roddenberry went on to study police work at Los Angeles City College until aviation captured his imagination, and he became a pilot through a civilian program with the United States Army Air Corps. At the start of World War II, he volunteered with the U.S. Army Air Forces and became a lieutenant, flying an estimated eighty-nine missions in the war. He was decorated with the Distinguished Flying Cross and the Air Medal.[3] After the war, he flew commercial flights for Pan Am, and over the years was involved in three plane crashes, leading him to become a crash investigator.

In 1947, Roddenberry was a passenger on a Pan Am flight that crashed in the Syrian desert, an experience that solidified his skeptical beliefs. He recalls:

> As we were coming down, and death was absolutely certain . . . I thought, maybe I ought to pray. I remember thinking, "Wait a minute." I didn't ordinarily pray, and I wouldn't have much respect for a god that would accept my prayers when I was in dire straits like this. He would be bound to judge you, if he's judging you, on

---

1. See TrekMovie.com Staff, "Alex Kurtzman Hopes," para. 6; and Arenas, "Star Trek Boss," para. 8.
2. Alexander, "Gene Roddenberry," 6.
3. Memory Alpha Wiki, "Gene Roddenberry," para. 7.

what you did in ordinary times. He just wouldn't accept prayers at times like this. I remember making up my mind not to pray. I thought, "OK, take me as I am." I've always been rather proud of that. If you believe something in a dire emergency, that is probably what you truly believe.[4]

Roddenberry helped the flight crew calm passengers as the plane came down, and he survived the crash with two broken ribs. He was able to pull a few passengers to safety away from the plane and procure first aid.[5]

The following year Roddenberry decided to leave aviation. He moved with his first wife to Los Angeles to try his hand at scriptwriting for the budding television industry. He then took a job as a Los Angeles police officer to pay the bills. Eventually, he became a communications officer and speechwriter for the chief of police.

He began writing scripts for television shows in the 1950s and 1960s, such as *Have Gun Will Travel* and *Bat Masterson*, and he produced pilots for several series that were not picked up by the networks. He then created a show called *The Lieutenant* which ran for one year, where he worked with actors who would eventually star on *Star Trek*, such as Leonard Nimoy, Nichelle Nichols, and Majel Barrett (whom he later married).

In 1964 he began work on *Star Trek* and pitched it to several networks. Desilu Studios, led at the time by Lucille Ball, finally consented to produce a *Star Trek* pilot. NBC liked the pilot but felt it was too intellectual for the average viewer. So the network ordered an unprecedented second pilot in 1965. It was then that NBC committed to the series, and it ran for three seasons from 1966–69. Though ratings seemed low for the show during its run, it became an enormous hit in the 1970s as it grew in syndication.

Roddenberry then created a second live *Trek* series, *Star Trek: The Next Generation*, in 1987. Like the first series, TNG was a remarkable success. He also wrote the story for *Star Trek: The Motion Picture* in 1979, which was a critical failure but made enough of a profit to warrant making further films. To date, thirteen *Trek* films have been made, with the "reboot" films of the franchise beginning in 2009.

Roddenberry saw *Star Trek* as a way to espouse his views, stating in his interview in *The Humanist* that "*Star Trek* is my statement to the world . . . [it] is more than just my political philosophy. It is my social philosophy, my

---

4. Alexander, *Star Trek Creator*, 86.
5. Alexander, *Star Trek Creator*, 87.

racial philosophy, my overview of life and the human condition."[6] While his controversial views were sometimes hampered by censors in the 1960s, with *Star Trek* he surreptitiously disguised his views as alien problems on other planets and was able to slip them past the censors.

RODDENBERRY AND SECULAR HUMANISM

In 1986 Roddenberry joined the *American Humanist Association*, publicly identified as a secular humanist, and was later awarded the Humanist Arts Award by the AHA.[7] He was against organized religion, he said, because he felt much of it was nonsense, and it could lead to senseless violence.[8] "How can I take seriously a god-image that requires that I prostrate myself every seven days and praise it? That sounds to me like a very insecure personality."[9] (We will see such an "insecure personality" in chapter 5.)

What is secular humanism? Humanism is related to atheism in that it assumes that God does not exist or he cannot be known (or is simply absent). According to secular humanism, since God is not there, he is not the foundation of moral values, nor is he needed for humans to be moral. In fact, according to humanism, humans have within themselves the ability to bring about complete peace: a lack of conflict between nation-states or groups of people, as well as an inner peace within individuals simply through their own internal resources.[10] Roddenberry identified with these beliefs and worked to weave them, often subtly, into his *Star Trek* scripts. In his interview with *The Humanist* a few months before his death in 1991, he admitted that he hid his humanist views early in his life so that he would not alienate his television audiences or the networks.[11]

He was open to the divine as long as it was not the traditional Judeo-Christian God. In a fascinating reflection on the world of *Trek*, he declared, "I've always assumed that by this time [the twenty-fourth century], there is a belief that is common to people in *Star Trek* that, yes, there is something

6. Alexander, "Gene Roddenberry," 14.

7. Alexander, "Gene Roddenberry," 5, 7.

8. On Roddenberry thinking religion was "nonsense," see Alexander, "Gene Roddenberry," 6–7. On his view that religion could lead to violence, see Cushman, *Voyages: TOS Season One*, 3.

9. Van Hise, *Roddenberry*, ch. 1, "Visionary in the Making."

10. See Flynn, "Secular Humanism Defined."

11. For more on this, see Alexander, "Gene Roddenberry," 7–8, 17–18.

out there. There is, perhaps, something that guides our lives, but we don't know what it is and we don't know *if* it is."[12]

He once wrote a letter to his Catholic cousin (no doubt attempting to soften his skeptical views): "I do not belong to any church, but I *do* consider myself a religious man. I believe that I am a part of you, and you are a part of me, and we are all a part of life . . . also a part of the creative force and intelligence behind life. Therefore, if we are a part of God then our lives are not brief, meaningless things, but rather have great importance and significance."[13] This is a type of pantheism, the view that "god" or the divine is part of the universe, and the universe is part of "god." It is a deification of nature. For Roddenberry, a deification of humanity.

Importantly, the year before he wrote this letter to his cousin in 1976, Roddenberry attacked the traditional concept of God, writing a scathing scene for the then-planned *Star Trek II* film. In the scene there is a transporter malfunction similar to the scene in *Star Trek: The Motion Picture*. Three people materialize in the transporter, but one person next to Kirk begins to contort, and horribly morphs into an unrecognizable blob of flesh. Screaming in terror, the tortured pile of flesh claws for its phaser, turns the phaser on itself, and fires, disappearing in a green flash of light. A shaken Kirk reports to the captain that one of the personnel beamed aboard has died. The captain, named Harcotte, says: "Yes. God used her to beam in at the transporter position you were to use. To demonstrate His presence to you." Another character adds, "To remind you that He can be a God of wrath as well as mercy."[14] Did Roddenberry believe the Christian God was this cruel and petty? Apparently. It seems he was attacking the theology of God's sovereignty here, in which God sometimes allows tragedies to happen for his greater purposes. (But since God is good, he *never* allows *senseless* suffering to occur, such as in this scene.)[15]

It is important to note these tensions between attacks on Christianity and a belief in the divine, because Kevin C. Neece, in his book *The Gospel According to Star Trek*, believes that Roddenberry's adherence to a divine presence makes him an "unusual theist" instead of an atheist or an agnostic. Neece declares: "It is possible that were [Roddenberry] helped

---

12. Alexander, "Gene Roddenberry," 28.
13. Alexander, *Star Trek Creator*, 423.
14. Cushman, *Voyages: 1970s Volume 2*, 41–42.
15. For an analysis of the problem of evil, see Craig and Moreland, *Philosophical Foundations*, 540–55.

to understand that the true gospel offered exactly the vision, hope and future for humankind that he sought, his theological perspective might have changed." This is true, of course, but Neece continues: "Ultimately, though, his heart seemed to be oriented toward the things of God and toward the heart of grace. That he rejected Christianity in name may not matter in the end."[16] This is unjustifiably optimistic, given that Roddenberry self-identified as a secular humanist and directly attacked the Christian conception of God on multiple occasions (in *Star Trek* and other places).

Thus, it is important to note that even though the term "atheist" is made up of the prefix "a," meaning "not," and "theist," meaning "God," many atheists today are not making a philosophical declaration about whether anything supernatural in the universe exists. Instead, for them, "atheist" is essentially a protest term. They are protesting the traditional concept of God and traditional religions as irrational or harmful to their adherents. Such atheists aren't necessarily declaring they think there is *nothing* divine out there.[17] Roddenberry himself talked about his *Star Trek* characters believing in "something out there" in the same *Humanist* interview in which he identified as a humanist. He certainly wouldn't have been disturbed to have been called an "atheist." But he would have been irritated at Neece's description of him as a person who "had a hunger in his heart for the culmination of salvation."[18]

Whether we label Roddenberry an atheist, an agnostic, or an unusual theist, matters little for our purposes here. The important thing is that he rejected the Christian God, thought most of the Bible was mythical, and believed that most people who followed organized religions were on some level being manipulated.[19] Organized religions, and Christianity in particular, were ridiculous to him and in some ways harmful. Roddenberry felt *Star Trek* was the perfect vehicle to air his religious views, as well as his other views about the world.

He also believed that the goodness of humankind would bring about a peaceful, just world. We see his humanist ideas in *Star Trek*'s vision of the future, in which hundreds of member worlds who are part of the United Federation of Planets have achieved peace between themselves, outgrown

---

16. Neece, *Gospel According to Star Trek*, 27.

17. See Kaur, "Why People Are Reluctant," sect. "What Do Atheists Believe?"

18. Neece, *Gospel According to Star Trek*, 26.

19. For Roddenberry's belief that religious believers are being manipulated, see Fern, *Gene Roddenberry*, 109–11.

war, and banished poverty. Violence, greed, and selfishness are things of the past. The ships of Starfleet represent a peaceful exploration of the galaxy: to "explore strange new worlds; to seek out new life forms and new civilizations."

"Gene felt strongly about the goodness of mankind," Rick Berman, an executive producer on *The Next Generation*, notes. "He knew there were rotten things [about mankind] also, but he liked to think of the future where wonderful things would continue and man could enhance the quality of his life."[20]

Roddenberry also believed that as civilizations evolved over time, they would leave myths and religious beliefs behind, and we see this in numerous *Trek* episodes. This, of course, is an idea from the Enlightenment: that the inevitable march of science would show religious myths, and all kinds of myths, to be false, primitive explanations. Thus, Roddenberry's secular humanism did make it into *Trek*. In many ways, *Star Trek* is a show that promotes an Enlightenment view of the world: a view in which science and reason show us what is real and solve whatever problems face humanity.

WHY DID RODDENBERRY PUT CHRISTIAN THEMES INTO *TREK*?

In spite of Roddenberry's secular beliefs, *Star Trek* has in the past and continues today to include various Christian themes and symbols. Surprisingly, this began with Roddenberry himself, who, even though he didn't believe in Christianity, included Christian ideas in *Trek* episodes like "Bread and Circuses" (TOS) and "Bem" (TAS). In 1964 when he pitched the new *Star Trek* series to the networks, among the story ideas he included was this: "THE COMING: Alien people in an alien society, but something disturbingly familiar about the quiet dignity of one who is being condemned to crucifixion."[21] In fact, Roddenberry was so successful in putting Christian themes into *Have Gun Will Travel* that he received an award from the American Baptist Convention for being among a few writers who were "consistently identifying themselves with the Christian way of life on radio and television."[22]

20. Van Hise, *Roddenberry*, ch. 12, "Final Bow."
21. Cushman, *Voyages: TOS Season One*, 23.
22. Cushman, *Voyages: TOS Season One*, 10.

As we will see, Alex Kurtzman has followed in Roddenberry's footsteps by continuing to explore Christian themes in new *Trek* episodes like "New Eden" (DIS), "Children of the Comet" (SNW), and "All Those Who Wander" (SNW).

Why did Roddenberry include Christian themes if he didn't believe in them? He admits that he wrote religious themes to please audiences and the censors. He often held back some of his more radical and skeptical ideas as he knew the networks or the public would not accept them. "I can remember going out of my way to not deal directly with what my thoughts were [about Christianity] for several reasons. I had learned early in school that the world was a cruel and difficult place, so I learned to cover myself. Perhaps I was consciously dishonest . . . "[23] But he felt that with *Star Trek: The Next Generation*, he was finally at liberty to explore all of his ideas without network interference.[24] TNG was syndicated and not network-based, but Roddenberry also felt that the TV audience had matured sufficiently to appreciate his undiluted views.

Interestingly, we will see that the *Trek* series created after Roddenberry died tended to be more positive about religious beliefs. We will also see that scriptwriters who wrote for *Star Trek* often put Christian symbolism into their stories.

Star Trek is not simply a humanist enterprise, it is much, much more. It is worth studying not only for its inclusion of Christian themes, but also because the secular themes in *Trek* make us think, reflect on the world around us, and contemplate how Christian ideas are related to these themes. *Star Trek* sharpens our thoughts about God, humankind, society, and theology, and for that we should be eternally grateful.

---

23. Alexander, "Gene Roddenberry," 7.
24. Alexander, "Gene Roddenberry," 12, 14.

SECTION II

Humanism in *Trek*

INTRODUCTION

As we saw in chapter 2, Gene Roddenberry embraced secular humanism and put humanist themes into *Star Trek*, especially *The Original Series* and *The Next Generation*. Later iterations of *Trek* would further his ideas. He believed that the God of the Bible was capricious and self-absorbed, and that organized religions manipulated their adherents. Such beliefs stunted humanity's progress. He also believed that primitive cultures would easily mistake advanced technology for the divine. Regarding the future, he created a *Trek* universe in which humankind had banished war, poverty, and discrimination. Human beings were their own best hope for a brighter future. These ideas laid the foundation for the episodes in this section.

As we will see, the *Discovery Short Trek* "The Brightest Star" exposes a technologically advanced race that uses religious beliefs to manipulate a more primitive race in order to consume them. In the TNG episode "Who Watches the Watchers," Starfleet anthropologists who are secretly observing a pre-warp society are discovered by the inhabitants of the planet and venerated as gods. And in "Who Mourns for Adonais?" (TOS), Kirk and crew meet the god Apollo, whom they discover is an alien who visited Greece thousands of years ago and became the basis for the Greek myths.

In these episodes, pay careful attention to issues of technology and superiority: How can the inhabitants of Saru's planet avoid religious manipulation? Do all religions manipulate their adherents? How might advanced

SECTION II: Humanism in *Trek*

technology mislead primitive cultures into worshipping those who have it? What precautions should Starfleet officers take to ensure this doesn't happen, and how does the Prime Directive, the rule of non-interference in developing cultures, help?[1]

The following episodes provoke fascinating questions about whether religious beliefs are true, whether they manipulate others, and whether science itself misleads people into believing in the divine. How do the ideas in these episodes conflict with Christianity or support it?

---

1. See the definition and discussion of the Prime Directive in ch. 4.

3

When the Quarry Questions
"The Brightest Star" (*Discovery*)

WATCH "THE BRIGHTEST STAR" (*STAR TREK: SHORT TREKS*, DIS SEASON 1)

"The Brightest Star" is a flashback explaining Commander Saru's origins and his journey to becoming a Starfleet officer on the USS *Discovery*. On his home planet of Kaminar, Saru's people, the Kelpiens, live a simple and agricultural life and strive to maintain the Great Balance, a religious harmony between them and the more advanced race which orbits the planet, the Ba'ul. The Great Balance preserves peace and abundant harvests for the Kelpiens. But when they reach the maturity of the Vahar'ai, a painful physiological change which they are taught is fatal, Kelpiens are required to report for a ceremony called the Culling, in which "chosen" Kelpiens offer themselves to the Ba'ul for "sustenance." They are beamed up to the Ba'ul ship, never to be seen again. The Kelpiens are taught that if they don't submit to the Culling, the Great Balance will be dissolved and will destroy all life on Kaminar. To keep the Kelpiens in line, the Ba'ul teach them that the Watchful Eye, which is really a network of technologically advanced sensors all over the planet, is ever present and must be appeased. Saru's father is one Kelpien priest among several thousand who cooperate with the Watchful Eye and preside over the Culling ceremonies.

As Saru matures, he begins to question his father about life beyond the stars. Is there a means to reach the stars like the Ba'ul have? Are there other advanced races besides the Ba'ul? Saru's father is adamant that Saru not ask such questions. "The Balance must not be upset!" he says. But Saru's curiosity is unsatiated.

During one culling, a piece of the Ba'ul ship breaks off, and Saru's father tells him to destroy it. But Saru secretly takes it, fixes it, and squirrels it away. He discovers a way to send a message on a broad beam out to the stars, and broadcasts a "Hello" to anyone who will listen. He receives a response, and one night a shuttlecraft booms out of warp and lands. We see a young Lt. Philippa Georgiou step out and invite Saru to go with her to join Starfleet. Saru steps into the shuttlecraft and leaves his family, never to return.

Importantly, we learn in the second-season episode "The Sound of Thunder" that the Vahar'ai transformation isn't terminal, that it actually frees Kelpiens from their crippling fear and makes them powerful, both physically and psychologically. Early in the history of Kaminar, after the Kelpiens emerged on the other side of their Vahar'ai, *they* were the predators preying on the Ba'ul. The Ba'ul lied to the Kelpiens to keep them weak and a constant source of food.

WORLDVIEW ANALYSIS

There are several humanist concepts in "The Brightest Star." The idea that organized religions are manipulative is illustrated in the story of the Ba'ul and the Kelpiens, as is the idea that it is forbidden to question long-held religious beliefs.

> **SARU'S FATHER:** The Balance must not be upset. Those who offer their lives do so so that the Ba'ul can be sustained! So that the rest of us may live in peace and comfort.

The Ba'ul perpetuated the lie of the Great Balance in order to make it easy to prey on the Kelpiens. Tragically, fear of upsetting the Balance kept the Kelpiens in line.

A number of *Star Trek* stories explore the issue of religious manipulation, and this scene is a deliberate nod to Gene Roddenberry's belief that organized religions are deceptive and controlling.¹ In a famous interview with Yvonne Fern (who is Catholic), Roddenberry declared:

> I condemn charlatans. I condemn false prophets. I condemn the effort to take away the power of rational decision, to drain people of their free will—and a hell of a lot of money in the bargain. That doesn't just apply to those religions you mentioned ["born-agains and evangelicals"]. It applies to your religion, and all religions who use the notion of God as a weapon against humanity.²

This is a strong statement, and Roddenberry attempts to soften it by declaring that Fern and other "intelligent" religious people are not taken in by "charlatans."³ But he clearly stereotypes most forms of Christianity (as well as other religions) as full of greedy, power-hungry leaders manipulating hapless followers.

IS CHRISTIANITY MANIPULATIVE?

Why did Roddenberry put traditional Christianity into the "manipulative" camp? He believed that Christian doctrines are logically incoherent and false, so he felt that *there must be* another reason people are teaching them. While his reasons are not entirely clear for concluding much of Christianity is manipulative, in an interview with David Alexander, Roddenberry hints at these reasons. He calls Baptist communion "phony," and later in the same interview he describes Christian doctrines as "largely nonsense" and "reaches of logic." This implies he feels Christian traditions are manipulative because they are based on obviously false doctrines.⁴ But why assume Christian doctrines are "reaches of logic"? It is clear he did not investigate such doctrines very carefully. He could have read fascinating defenses by the church fathers (leaders in the early centuries of Christianity) who wrote against such accusations, but by his own admission, he was uninterested to investigate such things.⁵ Therefore, he wasn't in a position to know whether classical Christian doctrines are false or not.

---

1. On new *Trek* series following Roddenberry's vision, see ch. 2.
2. Fern, *Gene Roddenberry*, 109–10. Despite Neece's description of how this excerpt from Roddenberry is sometimes misquoted, the atheistic force of the quotation stands. See Neece, *Gospel According to Star Trek*, 6–17, and see ch. 2.
3. Fern, *Gene Roddenberry*, 111.
4. Alexander, "Gene Roddenberry," 6–7.
5. Alexander, "Gene Roddenberry," 6.

SECTION II: HUMANISM IN *TREK*

It is simply wrong to stereotype Christians (and other religions) as Roddenberry does. In fact, the Bible agrees that the kind of religious manipulation he abhors is nearly inevitable. "Watch out for false prophets. They come to you in sheep's clothing, but inwardly they are ferocious wolves. By their fruit you will recognize them," Jesus said (Matt 7:15–16). The apostle Paul is even more specific:

> I urge you, brothers and sisters, to watch out for those who cause divisions and put obstacles in your way that are contrary to the teaching you have learned. Keep away from them. *For such people are not serving our Lord Christ, but their own appetites. By smooth talk and flattery they deceive the minds of naïve people.* (Rom 16:17–18, emphasis mine)

The Bible warns against false teachers who twisted the apostles' teaching for their own gain. Some of these teachers followed the apostles from city to city, attempting to arrest and lead astray new congregations that Paul and other church leaders planted (see for example Acts 17:13–15). Others simply changed the apostles' teaching from within their own churches. "Such men are false apostles [and] deceitful workers," Paul declares (2 Cor 11:13).

Paul is confident that they were "deceitful workers" because he was careful to check his own teaching about Jesus with the apostles in Jerusalem, to make sure he wasn't contradicting the apostles' experiences of Jesus. Such apostles (who knew Jesus personally) followed rabbinic tradition and carefully memorized his deeds and teachings and passed them on to others. Since these memorized teachings were commonly known in Christian communities of the time, any serious deviation from them would have been recognized and corrected. As well, there were many followers of Jesus (besides the apostles) who knew him and his teaching during his lifetime, and they would have corrected divergent teachings as well.[6] Since Paul was not an original follower of Jesus, he checked his teaching with those who were. He describes his journey to Jerusalem to compare his teaching with the apostles' in Gal 1:18—2:5.

When Paul and the apostles call some teachers "false apostles" and "deceitful workers," are they simply making a power play for their own gain, declaring that whatever Christian factions they disagreed with were manipulative and deceptive? Some scholars have proffered this idea,[7] but

---

6. Komoszewski et al., *Reinventing Jesus*, 29–38.
7. See for example Pagels, *Gnostic Gospels*, xiii–xxxvi.

there is no evidence for such a claim. Despite what Elaine Pagels argues, there were no "competing Christianities" that arose at the same time as orthodox Christianity. Instead, there were deviant doctrines which were parasitic on the earlier, orthodox Christian beliefs. We know this because none of these "competing Christianities" date to the first century, as the New Testament documents do.[8]

Are religious people particularly naïve and susceptible to manipulation? Roddenberry seemed to think so. In his interview with Fern, he said, "For most of these poor devils, [religion] is nothing more than a substitute brain . . . And a malfunctioning one at that."[9]

No doubt some religious believers *are* naïve and easily led astray, but it doesn't follow that all are, or even the majority are. The only way to come to such a conclusion would be to assume, as Roddenberry does, that most religious doctrines are nonsensical and thus false. This would mean that, *necessarily*, for someone to believe them they must set aside their reason. But we've already seen that he is not in a position to know whether such doctrines are false. The idea here that most religious believers are naïve exemplifies a logical fallacy known as the fallacy of composition. This error makes an assumption about a whole group based on some part of the whole. For example: "Because some evangelicals bomb abortion clinics, all evangelicals must be terrorists." It's simply a stereotype.

In an important sense, then, this episode of *Discovery* is a warning against religious manipulation and a reminder that we need to use reason and evidence to sift through religious claims to see if they have merit or are deceptive. The Bible agrees that wherever religious beliefs are found, charlatans and deceivers will be among them, trying to control others and lie for their own purposes, including financial gain. But the Bible does not assume, as Roddenberry does, that such deceivers exemplify Christianity. Instead, such teachers are outliers. The savvy believer will recognize these teachers, see through their deception, and not be led astray.

IS GOD LIKE THE WATCHFUL EYE?

SARU'S FATHER: The Watchful Eye rules the skies.

---

8. For a scholarly defense, see Yamauchi, *Pre-Christian Gnosticism*. For a popular summary of such arguments, see Bock, *Missing Gospels*.

9. Fern, *Gene Roddenberry*, 111.

SECTION II: Humanism in *Trek*

In this scene, Saru's father defends the Great Balance and reaffirms that the whole planet is monitored by the Watchful Eye. Saru is not to ask questions about what is beyond the sky and how to get there because "If the Great Balance had meant for us to fly, we would have been given wings." All Saru needs to know is that the Watchful Eye is in the sky and monitors its people.

Does God keep watch over us like the police sometimes do, endeavoring to keep us in line? Is he like the Watchful Eye? The Bible *does* say that wherever we are, we cannot get away from God:

> Where shall I go from your Spirit? Or where shall I flee from your presence? If I ascend to heaven, you are there . . . If I take the wings of the morning and dwell in the uttermost parts of the sea, even there your hand shall lead me, and your right hand shall hold me. (Ps 139:7–10 ESV)

As well, Paul says in 1 Cor 4:5 that God "will bring to light what is hidden in darkness and expose the motives of the heart." Does this mean that God watches people because he likes to catch them in wrongdoing? Does he have nothing better to do?

The truth is, God watches over his people because he *loves* them, not because he is policing their behavior. In the quote above from Ps 139, David says, "Even there your hand shall lead me, your right hand shall hold me." This is an image of God's immediate, loving presence to guide and protect his people wherever they go. It amplifies an earlier phrase in the psalm, "You lay your hand upon me." According to Willem VanGemeren, "The placement of the divine hand signifies protection and blessing."[10] In this psalm, there is nowhere God's people can flee from his loving presence and guidance, not the greatest heights nor the lowest depths. Even if we think we have escaped his love, we have not.

Additionally, since God loves his people, he watches over them to *protect* them from sin, which harms them and others. While the passage in 1 Cor 4:5 indicates God will judge all people's actions and motives, in the context Paul is warning the Corinthians not to make judgments *themselves* about whether a person is righteous. It's an encouragement to love others and not judge them, since God will judge their actions himself. Living in fear of God's "watchful eye" is not in view here.

---

10. See VanGemeren, *Psalms*, Ps 139:1–6. VanGemeren cross references Gen 48:14, 17, and Exod 33:22.

We need to remember that later in 1 Cor 13, when Paul defines love, he is also describing God's character. God is primarily a God of love. We see this clearly in 1 John 4:

> God is love. Whoever lives in love lives in God, and God in them. This is how love is made complete among us so that we will have confidence on the day of judgment: In this world we are like Jesus. There is no fear in love. But perfect love drives out fear, because fear has to do with punishment. The one who fears is not made perfect in love. (1 John 4:16–18)

Everyone who has trusted Christ's sacrifice for their sins and accepted God's forgiveness can have complete confidence on the day of judgment, because God's love covers them with Christ's sacrifice. God will pronounce judgment at the end of time, but only because he must, not because he enjoys it. Speaking of God's judgment of Israel for its sins, when he allowed his people to be sent into captivity, Lam 3:33 says, "For he does not willingly bring affliction or grief to anyone." As well, Ezek 33:11 says, "As surely as I live, declares the Sovereign Lord, I take no pleasure in the death of the wicked, but rather that they turn from their ways and live. Turn! Turn from your evil ways!" God does not enjoy judgment, according to these verses. He only punishes sin because justice requires it. He is not gleefully policing us to catch us in wrongdoing.

Thus, God's judgment is not the primary reason he is present with us. He is present with us because *he simply likes being with us*. We know this from Eph 1:18, which declares God has a rich inheritance *in us*. Note that this verse is not describing *our* inheritance *in him*, but *his* inheritance *in us*, a remarkable truth.

In "The Brightest Star," the Watchful Eye scrutinizes every action, every behavior of the Kelpiens, so the Ba'ul can control them. But that is not why God watches us. He watches us because he loves us and wants to protect us.

IS IT WRONG TO DOUBT YOUR FAITH?

SARU'S FATHER: That is the Balance. That is how it has always been. And you will question it no more.

Again, Saru's father tells him that the Great Balance is the way things are and cannot be changed. Saru is not to ask any questions about it but just submit to it.

Is it a sin to doubt your faith? Saru's father certainly thought so. He suppressed Saru's beautifully inquisitive mind.

What does Scripture say about doubting your faith? In James it says:

> When you ask [God for wisdom], you must believe and not doubt, because the one who doubts is like a wave of the sea, blown and tossed by the wind. That person should not expect to receive anything from the Lord. Such a person is double-minded and unstable in all they do. (Jas 1:6–8)

Sometimes verses like this are misused to say that if you have even the tiniest bit of doubt, you are in sin and God will do nothing for you. But that's not what this verse says. This is about trusting God as a person, not doubting Christian doctrine. God's people are not to doubt his *generosity*; if they need wisdom, he will simply give it. *He loves giving.*[11] As Vouga says, the theme of the book of James is "the prodigality of God."[12] The context here is about God giving wisdom in his generosity, not believing whether Christianity is true. It's as if James is saying, "If you don't believe God is generous, why are you asking?" This fits with the parable of the talents in Matt 25:14–30. A master leaves his servants and asks them to invest his money while he is gone. The servant in the story whom the master rebukes is the one who feared his master was "a hard man" so he didn't invest any of the master's money. In other words, he didn't think the master was trustworthy.

What about verses that say to believe and not doubt? James says, "When you ask you must not doubt," and Jesus said, "If anyone says to this mountain, 'Go, throw yourself into the sea,' and does not doubt in their heart but believes that what they say will happen, it will be done for them" (Mark 11:23). Many interpreters have taken these verses to mean that if a person suppresses all conscious doubt and wills himself to believe, God will do what he asks. But is that what these verses actually mean?

Speaking again of the passage in James, George Stulac declares:

> A further distortion of the Biblical teaching occurs when Christians treat James' warning against doubt (and the similar teaching of Jesus in Matt 21:21) superficially, taking it to require a willful

---

11. See Stulac, *James*, 41–43.
12. Martin, *James*, 18.

suppression of mental doubts. This can become an unrecognized attempt to manipulate God by one's own power of positive thinking. The error has left many in bondage to fear, afraid of their own thoughts and afraid of the God who might hold their doubts against them and therefore not grant them the wisdom needed. The result is a crippling of people's faith and a perversion of the very truth James is teaching: that God gives freely without finding fault.[13]

Jesus and James are not giving technical descriptions of how much faith a person must have before God will act on their behalf. Rather, these verses are saying that God is trustworthy, so his followers can trust him to be good and give them what they need. We need to remember that God is a person, not a machine that dispenses miracles if we muster up enough faith. If we come to him with our doubts, God will have compassion on us because that's simply who he is.

This fits with Matt 17:20, in which Jesus said that if you have faith "as small as a mustard seed" (one of the tiniest seeds in the Middle East), "you can say to this mountain: Move . . . and it will move." The mountains move, not because God's people have achieved a certain threshold of faith, but simply because God hears them, and he is all-powerful. He *wants* to respond.

We see God's graciousness with people who doubt in passages such as Genesis 15, where God said to Abraham, "I am your shield and your very great reward," and Abraham responded, "What can you give me since I remain childless and the one who will inherit my estate is Eliezer of Damascus?" (Gen 15:1–2). Incredibly, Abraham said "What can you give me?" *after* God had already promised him a son (in Gen 12). In other words, Abraham brought his doubts to God, and God responded with compassion, solidifying his promise to Abraham with a solemn oath. He didn't rebuke Abraham or say, "If you don't have enough faith, I won't give you a son." He responded with grace.

We also see this grace in Jesus' response to Thomas' famous doubts about Jesus' resurrection. Thomas had said that he would not believe Jesus was raised unless he could "see the nail marks in his hands and put my finger where the nails were." Jesus did not rebuke Thomas for his lack of faith, but showed him his hands, his feet, and his side, and Thomas believed. Jesus then said that people who believe, without seeing like Thomas did,

---

13. Stulac, *James*, 42.

are blessed (John 20:24–29). We also see a gracious response from Jesus when a man came to him with a son who was possessed by a demon. The father said to Jesus, "If you can do anything, take pity on us!" Jesus replied, "'If you can?' Everything is possible for one who believes." The boy's father exclaimed, "I do believe; help me overcome my unbelief!" (Mark 9:23–24). Jesus then healed his son, even though the father's faith was wavering.

These examples indicate that, in general, it's not wrong to doubt. It's wrong to doubt God and *walk away*. When a person doubts, they are to come to God with their doubts. That's faith. In fact, we can make a good case that the Scriptures usually don't warn us against doubt per se, as much as they warn us against not trusting God himself. Faith is usually about trusting a person, not a set of concepts. Yes, some passages indicate we must trust a doctrine or a concept, such as Matt 8:26, where Jesus rebuked the disciples for being afraid they would drown in a storm. After he calmed the storm, he *did* rebuke them for not believing that the Messiah had authority over nature. But note again, this is not a passage encouraging us to muster up faith to force God's hand to act. Instead, Jesus simply rebuked them for not having faith at *all* (see Mark 4:40). That is, Jesus was not talking about the strength of their faith here, but that they simply didn't believe he had power over nature.[14]

In summary, God met the doubts of Abraham, Thomas, and others with gracious understanding. When he said, "Have faith and do not doubt in your heart," he was not talking about doubting Christian concepts or doctrinal truth. He meant we should not doubt that he, as a generous parent, would give us everything we need. Jesus specifically addressed this in Matt 7, where he spoke of God answering our prayers: "Ask and it will be given to you . . . knock and the door will be opened to you . . . If you then, though you are evil, know how to give good gifts to your children, how much more will your Father in heaven give good gifts to those who ask him!" (Matt 7:7–11).

Returning to Saru's dilemma in "The Brightest Star," it is interesting to speculate: If he had been allowed to ask questions of his faith, would he have felt the need to leave Kaminar to get answers? Did his father's closed-mindedness drive Saru away? We may never know for sure. But we do know that it's never wrong to ask honest questions of God.

---

14. See Hagner, *Matthew 1–13*, 222.

4

Dark Ages or Enlightenment?
"Who Watches the Watchers" (*The Next Generation*)

WATCH "WHO WATCHES THE WATCHERS" (TNG SEASON 3)

In this episode, the *Enterprise* speeds to planet Mintaka III to rescue a group of Starfleet anthropologists who have been secretly surveying the planet's primitive inhabitants. Their observation post, a duck blind which is digitally hidden from the primitive people there, becomes visible when its reactor explodes, injuring the scientists. In their haste to evacuate the scientists, the *Enterprise* crew fails to see a local inhabitant named Liko climb up to see the now visible outpost and become injured when he falls from the rock face. Dr. Crusher quickly evacuates him to sickbay and keeps him sedated there so he will not see the ship's technology, which would violate the Prime Directive. But unbeknownst to her, he awakes and sees Captain Picard talk to patients in sickbay. When Liko is mended and secretly beamed back to the surface, he tells the inhabitants there that a god named "The Picard" healed him. Mintakan myth already included a god called "The Overseer," so Liko concludes that "The Picard" must be the ancient Overseer. When he returns to the planet, Liko is able to convince his friends this is true.

But things get complicated when Liko and the villagers capture Counselor Troi, who had beamed down to the planet with Riker, both disguised as Mintakans, to secretly beam up an injured Federation scientist. Through a series of events in which Liko and the villagers are afraid they have angered "The Picard," they wonder if they should kill the captured Troi to placate him.

Hearing all this from Troi's subcutaneous communicator, Picard calls a conference on the *Enterprise* with his officers and the anthropologists to figure out what to do. The head anthropologist, Dr. Barron, says that Picard must beam down and pretend to be the Overseer because the planet has already been culturally contaminated anyway, and that's the only way he can repair the damage. But Picard is adamant that he cannot impersonate a god and sabotage the "achievement" of the Mintakans, who have left primitive, superstitious religion behind. He decides to beam up Nuria, the leader of the villagers, and show her that the "magic" of "The Picard" is just advanced technology. He succeeds in convincing Nuria that even though the *Enterprise* is amazing, the crew are just physical beings like her. But when she and Picard return to the planet, the villagers are still trying to decide whether to kill Troi to please "The Picard." Liko sees Picard, and to prove he is a god, Liko shoots him with an arrow thinking it won't hurt him. But Picard goes down. Grieved when he sees Picard bleeding like a Mintakan would, he and the villagers realize Picard is merely a mortal like they are. A healed Picard then explains what the scientists have been doing there, and the *Enterprise* leaves orbit.

WORLDVIEW ANALYSIS

"Who Watches the Watchers" is a translation of the Latin phrase "*Quis custodiet ipsos custodes?*" It means "Who will guard the guards themselves?" or "Who will watch the watchmen?" The phrase first appears in *Satires*, a collection of poems by the Roman poet Juvenal, which dates from the first to second centuries A.D.

In this episode, "Who Watches the Watchers" has a double meaning. First, during the story, the Mintakans become aware of the Starfleet anthropologists, who are "watching" them, and thus the Mintakan culture is contaminated. Once Mintakans can "watch" the "watchers," they don't know what to believe about themselves or their society. But the second meaning would refer to Starfleet itself as a "watcher of the watchers." Starfleet is responsible for making sure its own members, especially the crews of starships on exploratory missions, do not contaminate the growth of less-developed societies. This is a rule Starfleet enforces known as the "Prime Directive" (discussed in more detail below). Thus, the Federation has its own rules in place to "watch the watchers."

In this chapter we will explore the two main themes in this episode: how to follow the Prime Directive and why it is important, and second, the idea that religious beliefs are from the "Dark Ages," full of superstition and ignorance. According to the script, superstitious and ignorant cultures would see advanced technology and think it is magic. But all this is based on stereotypes of "primitive" peoples, as well as stereotypes of what happened between science and Christianity in the Middle Ages.

THE PRIME DIRECTIVE

CRUSHER: Before you start quoting me the Prime Directive, he'd already seen us. The damage was done. It was either bring [Liko] aboard or let him die.

PICARD: Then why didn't you let him die?

CRUSHER: Because we were responsible for his injuries.

Much of the plot in this episode has to do with upholding the Prime Directive, the Starfleet rule that it is wrong to interfere with the growth of less technologically developed societies (a rule also known as General Order One). In this scene, we see the knotty problems for following the Prime Directive that resulted when Dr. Crusher beamed Liko aboard to save him. When he is healed in sickbay, Liko believes the god "Picard" healed him.

In spite of the precautions that Starfleet has taken to hide their existence from the Mintakans, contamination of Mintakan culture happens anyway. First, the reactor that camouflages the "duck blind" goes out, revealing the observation post. And second, in this scene in sickbay, after Picard asks Crusher why she didn't let Liko die, he tells her to wipe Liko's memory. But since Mintakans have a different brain chemistry, a memory wipe is impossible. Unbeknownst to Crusher, Liko wakes up in sickbay and sees the "magic" technology. This is a textbook case of why the Prime Directive is needed in the first place, and how hard it is *not* to contaminate cultures, even when all possible precautions are taken.

SECTION II: HUMANISM IN *TREK*

The Prime Directive is an important part of the Federation's moral code and is a prominent feature in many *Trek* episodes. Producer Gene Coon invented the idea when he rewrote the TOS script for "The Return of the Archons" (see chapter 12 for a discussion of this episode). In his rewrite he also allowed a loophole: The Directive only applies to "living, growing cultures."[1] This loophole allowed Captain Kirk to break the Directive in *The Original Series* and interfere with stagnant cultures when he thought it necessary, in episodes such as "Archons," "A Private Little War," and "The Apple."

As the concept of the Directive grew over time, we came to learn more about it from different *Trek* characters. Kirk once declared that "A starship captain's most solemn oath is that he will give his life, even his entire crew, rather than violate the Prime Directive."[2] Later Picard elaborated on the reasons behind the order: "The Prime Directive is not just a set of rules; it is a philosophy. . . and a very correct one. History has proven again and again that whenever mankind interferes with a less developed civilization, no matter how well-intentioned that interference may be, the results are invariably disastrous."[3]

However, there is an ongoing debate among *Star Trek* scholars about whether the Prime Directive is a hard-and-fast rule, or whether there are conditions under which it might be broken. David Kyle Johnson argues that a "stagnant culture" is not a good reason to interfere in a society as Kirk often does, since calling it "stagnant" is often simply imposing Western values of creativity and technological advance on non-Western societies. Are such values necessary for a culture to thrive? Johnson argues they are not, and he thinks it is immoral for Kirk to interfere in many of the TOS episodes in which he does. For example, Johnson argues that in the TOS episode "The Apple," there is a thriving culture even though it fits Kirk's definition of "stagnant."[4]

But Johnson goes on to say that often in contemporary discussions of cultural interference, a type of "cultural moral relativism" is defended, which states that "it is always wrong for one culture to impose its values on

1. Cushman, *Voyages: TOS Season One*, 489.
2. Kirk in "Omega Glory" (TOS season 2).
3. Picard in "Symbiosis" (TNG season 1).
4. See Johnson, "Prime Directive." Also, see vol. 2, ch. 6 for a discussion of "The Apple."

another."[5] He says, of course, it *is often* wrong to interfere in other cultures because what is thought of as "moral codes" are simply cultural conventions, such as how to dress or what is considered rude. In these cases, it is wrong to impose cultural changes from the outside, as has often been done in the past.

However, Johnson argues that cultural moral relativism cannot apply in every case because there are significant exceptions. What if another culture kidnaps people and enslaves them? Or a culture believes that rape is ethical? In such cases, it is obvious that cultural interference would be necessary because it is always wrong to do such things, regardless of whether a culture allows them. Thus, he argues that often cultural interference is morally wrong. But in a few cases in which moral values transcend cultures, it is allowed.[6]

THE PRIME DIRECTIVE AND VIRTUE ETHICS

Bárcenas and Bein, in their study of the Prime Directive, agree it is not a precise hard-and-fast rule, and that there are some cases in which the Directive needs to be broken. But how to know when to break it? Here they bring in virtue ethics: ethical theories which state that a virtuous person simply knows the right thing to do, based on their character. Both Confucius (551–479 BC) and Aristotle (384–322 BC) agree that "morality isn't as exact as mathematics, but it has a precision of its own."[7] What is morally right to do in a situation often isn't as precise as following an equation, but a person of virtue should be able to simply *see* the correct moral path.

Thus, according to virtue ethics, the emphasis is not so much on acting rightly or following a code of ethics (although this is included), but on becoming a person of character who instinctively knows the right thing to do in various situations. Interestingly, in (Western) virtue theory, which goes back to Plato and Aristotle, a "virtue" is a habit or disposition that rightly allows the person to flourish according to their nature, or "essence." While a complete description of virtue ethics is beyond the scope of this book, a "nature," defined as an "essence," is a set of essential properties that makes a thing what it is. An entity must have these properties, or it will

---

5. Johnson, "Prime Directive."
6. Johnson, "Prime Directive."
7. Bárcenas and Bein, "Make It So," 41. For a discussion of Confucius and virtue theory see Wong, "Chinese Ethics," sect. "2.1 Virtue Ethics."

cease to exist. An "accidental" property is a property that is not necessary for an entity to exist. For example, redness is an accidental property of a ball. A ball could be green and still be a ball. But roundness is an essential property of being a ball. If a ball is not round, it is no longer a ball. Regarding humans, Socrates could have black hair or blond hair, and still be the same person inside, still be Socrates. The color of his hair is an accidental property. But his humanness is part of his essence, and if he ceased to be "human," he would no longer be Socrates.[8]

In virtue theory, an essence has an end purpose or goal, a reason for which it exists. It is the *flourishing*, or *proper functioning* of that thing. For example, roundness is a property essential to a properly functioning ball. Without roundness, a ball is useless, or dysfunctional. Greenness is not necessary for the proper functioning of a ball, therefore it is an accidental property. A "flourishing" ball is one that has the right amount of air in it and the right amount of roundness for it to function well.

As Christian thinkers incorporated virtue theory into their theology, acting virtuously fulfilled God's design for human beings. Included is the idea that originally God did not design humans to sin, so a "vice" does not allow a person to function and flourish as they were designed. As well, virtues and vices apply not only to moral decisions, but to simple proper functioning. For example, "to study" is "a discipline that strengthens the mind and enriches the soul," thus it is an "intellectual virtue."[9]

On this view, acting virtuously regarding the Prime Directive would include a thorough understanding of the Directive and its purposes for preserving cultures (an intellectual virtue), and balancing these purposes with contrary considerations in which it may be necessary to bend or break the Directive to preserve a culture (which is a *moral* virtue). For example, in the TNG episode "Homeward," Picard and crew watch a planet's atmosphere irretrievably degrade, suffocating its entire population. But they refuse to interfere because of the Prime Directive. They are so set on following the Directive to the letter that a whole people dies and their culture with them.[10] A virtuous person would see that in this case, if the whole population dies, the purpose of the Directive is not fulfilled, since the culture also dies with it. Isn't an altered culture better than no culture at all?

---

8. For this summary of virtue ethics, see Craig and Moreland, *Philosophical Foundations*, 468–71. For a scholarly discussion of virtue ethics, see Adams, *Theory of Virtue*.
9. Moreland, *Love Your God*, 111.
10. Gregory, *Star Trek: Parallel Narratives*, 171.

According to virtue theory, a starship captain should not only be trained in leadership and command decisions, but in developing the kind of character that can simply see how best to serve a newly discovered culture. A virtuous person puts the culture's needs before their own personal needs or the needs of the Federation. Such a person would also know whether breaking the Directive is truly necessary to preserve a culture. With the exception of the episode above, Captain Picard typically has the character necessary to see how to serve newly discovered cultures, with or without the Prime Directive. But Kirk often imposes Western values on societies for his own or his crew's benefit, in episodes such as "A Private Little War" (TOS), where McCoy argues to uphold the Directive but Kirk declines to follow it.[11] To summarize, Starfleet Academy should either recruit only virtuous cadets, or train incoming cadets to become people of high character. (It should be noted that in Christian theology there is a type of external righteousness that can be defined as "high character," described in such Old Testament passages as Job chapter 1 (see Job 1:1, 8, 22). However, moral *perfection* is necessary to be in God's full presence, a higher standard which is only possible through a gift of God's grace).[12]

DOES ADVANCED TECHNOLOGY APPEAR DIVINE TO PRIMITIVE CULTURES?

> LIKO: Fento, you know the legends better than anyone. Do they not speak of beings like the kind I've seen?
>
> OJI: Who could vanish like smoke?
>
> FENTO: There are the stories of the Overseer who could appear and disappear at will.

There are several themes from secular humanism in "Who Watches the Watchers." Recall from chapter 2 that secular humanism believes that as humans develop over time, they will leave superstitious religious beliefs behind as science continues to triumph.

Consequently, one of the main themes of "Watchers" is that, to primitive people, the *Enterprise* and its workings appear to be magic. Here, Liko's daughter Oji refers to transporting as "vanishing like smoke," and Riker describes it as being "magically transformed to another place." Picard

---

11. See Johnson, "Prime Directive."
12. For righteousness as a free gift, see Paul's argument in Rom 8.

describes Nuria as believing "The Picard is a magical figure." And when Picard is soft-lit in sickbay, giving him an aura, this implies that futuristic technology (in this case, the lighting) would appear divine and magical to someone who didn't understand it.

Sci-fi writer Arthur C. Clarke famously stated this in his third law: "Any sufficiently advanced technology is indistinguishable from magic."[13] Michael Shermer later modified Clarke's law: "Any sufficiently advanced extraterrestrial intelligence is indistinguishable from God."[14] We know Clarke's ideas had a tremendous influence on the development of *Star Trek* because Gene Roddenberry frequently talked about it. He explained, "Arthur literally made my *Star Trek* idea possible, including the television series, the films . . . My association with the Clarke mind and concepts began in 1964 with his book *Profiles of the Future* . . . "[15] We can certainly see the third law in this story, especially when the advanced technology in sickbay, as magical as it is to Liko, makes him think Picard is a god.

While it is certainly possible that advanced technology, to a primitive culture, might be perceived as magic, it is the height of presumption to think that "primitive" people would not understand it also as a technology. "Primitives" are not as ignorant as some secular humanists believe. For example, when Europeans brought guns to the New World, Native Americans thought they were magic at first. But they soon learned to see them as simply a different technology that could help them fight on par with the Europeans, as well as hunt better. They adroitly traded with Europeans to acquire them.[16] We do a disservice to the Native Americans of that era when we assume they could not understand a new technology such as a rifle.

IS CHRISTIANITY SUPERSTITIOUS?

> PICARD: Millennia ago, [the Mintakans] abandoned their belief in the supernatural. Now you are asking me to sabotage that achievement, to send them back into the Dark Ages of superstition and ignorance and fear?

---

13. Clarke, *Profiles of the Future*, 34, 36.

14. Shermer, "Shermer's Last Law," 33.

15. Clarke, "How Arthur C. Clarke." Clarke's third law first appeared in a letter from Clarke to *Science* magazine in 1968. See Clarke, "Clarke's Third Law on UFOs."

16. See Silverman, "Guns, Empires and Indians," paras. 7–10.

These words of Picard articulate the central theme of the episode. He refuses the request of Dr. Barron to beam down to the Mintakans and impersonate a god because he believes the fact that they have left supernatural beliefs behind is an "achievement."

There are several things here to discuss. First, we see a highly negative characterization of the supernatural. The implication is that only ignorant people believe in such things, and smart, scientific people do not. It's worth highlighting again that Roddenberry rejected revealed Christianity because it was full of "largely magic, superstitious things," exactly the kind of beliefs that made it into this story. He rejected "the superstitious trappings of all organized religions,"[17] and we certainly see that here.

But why presume that smart, scientific people don't believe in organized religion? Thousands of scientists today identify as Christian, and nearly half identify with some type of organized religion. Elaine Howard Ecklund, a sociologist at Rice University, found that nearly 50 percent of American scientists believe in some form of religious tradition, and 25 percent of these identify as Christian. Only 34 percent of those surveyed considered themselves atheists.[18] It's clearly not the case that as science has progressed, religious beliefs have disappeared, even among scientists. Nor is there any indication that religious beliefs will disappear in the future.

When Picard implies that religious beliefs are based on "superstition and ignorance," what exactly does he mean? "Superstition" typically refers to an overly credulous belief in the supernatural, or an unverified belief that supernatural forces are behind certain events in nature. In other words, it's a supernatural belief based on little or no evidence. But Picard implies that all supernatural beliefs are superstitious because he does not look into the evidence for the Mintakan religion to see if it is rational to believe. If he had, this would have demonstrated that he thought there was evidence that justified *some* religious beliefs and not others. He also does not qualify his description of "ignorance, fear," or the "Dark Ages" by saying *some* of what was believed in the "Dark Ages" was true. He therefore paints religious beliefs with a broad (fictitious) brush. The term "superstitious," then, does not describe *any* religious belief, but an overly credulous belief.

---

17. See ch. 2, and Van Hise, *Roddenberry*, ch. 12, "Final Bow."

18. While the percentage of atheists and agnostics among scientists is higher than the general population, the number of traditionally religious scientists is surprisingly high at 48 percent. See Ecklund, *Science vs Religion*, 6, 33–34.

Many people today regard belief in the resurrection of Jesus as "superstitious." After all, dead men don't rise from the dead. But why assume it's a superstitious belief? Is it superstitious because there were no scientists there to verify it? Or is it superstitious because people of the day supposedly didn't believe in science, and thus were more likely to believe in the supernatural? But why assume the latter? People in the first century *knew* that dead people don't rise. When they treated the body with spices and buried it themselves, they knew it would have a strong stench in a few days. Such a person wasn't coming back.

But the biblical story describes Jesus appearing over a period of forty days to his disciples after he died. Not simply in visions, but physical manifestations (Acts 1:3, John 20:24–29, and Luke 24:13–32). For an ancient person that counted as evidence, and it should count as evidence today.[19] The people who saw the resurrected Jesus over this forty-day period were in his inner circle. They knew him the best and were the least likely to be fooled. So, while it may be superstitious to believe in the resurrection based on hearsay, the people who first taught it were in the best position of anyone to know whether it was true. At least for them, belief in the resurrection was not superstitious.

This could certainly be true for other supernatural events, which in fact *did* have enough evidence for them to be rationally believed by *eyewitnesses*. (For example, if a person believes in the resurrection, or a miracle, by hearing it third or fourth hand, this could constitute a superstitious belief. But if they hear it third or fourth hand simultaneously with the conviction of the Holy Spirit that the testimony is true, this would not constitute a superstitious belief.)[20]

It's worth noting here that one of the reasons Picard's speech about the Dark Ages and superstition is so compelling and feels true in the scene, is that we viewers know the Mintakan religion is fictitious; we know it was a myth created for this story. So of course, we know the Mintakan religion is false, undoubtedly full of ignorance and superstition. But the script connects the Mintakan myth to Earth, and specifically Christianity, by using the term "Dark Ages." When Picard uses that phrase, he connects our knowledge that the Mintakan religion is a myth to Christianity, which, he assumes, must also be a myth. Thus, something so obviously false (the Mintakan religion) fits nicely with the term "Dark Ages."

---

19. For detailed arguments on the resurrection, see ch. 10.
20. See Plantinga's theory in his *Warranted Christian Belief*, 241–89.

Dark Ages or Enlightenment?

SCIENCE AND CHRISTIANITY IN THE MIDDLE AGES

Let's look at Picard's phrase, "the Dark Ages of superstition, ignorance, and fear" in more detail. When he uses this phrase, Picard is assuming what is called the *conflict hypothesis,* the idea that science and religion have always been at war, and that science has triumphed. On this view, religious authorities in the Middle Ages arrested and persecuted scientists, but now that the scientific age has triumphed, religious beliefs have been shown to be inferior and superstitious. This view became popular in the late nineteenth century and still holds sway today. Interestingly, today's historians of science never use the term "Dark Ages" because it is misleading. And they believe almost no evidence supports the conflict hypothesis.[21]

For example, according to the conflict hypothesis scientists were routinely arrested and either tortured or burned at the stake in the "Dark Ages." In fact, *no scientists* were killed for their scientific beliefs. People that were burned at the stake were executed for heretical theological beliefs, not scientific ones. This was horrible, of course, but the point is that it was not scientists who were persecuted, but theologians. The only possible exception to this was Giordano Bruno, who did believe in a heliocentric universe. Scholars today are not sure why he was prosecuted as it's not clear from the records, but it is believed that he was arrested for starting a new neo-Platonic religion. In other words, he was not burned at the stake for his scientific beliefs, but most likely for his religious ones.[22]

As well, it is commonly thought today that Galileo was imprisoned and tortured for his support of Copernicus' view that the Earth revolved around the sun. It is true that he was arrested for giving evidence that the Earth moved, against the so-called evidence in Scripture that it was stationary. (Scriptures that appear to support a stationary Earth include Ps 104:5, Ps 75:3, and 1 Chr 16:30. But as Galileo and others pointed out, often the Bible speaks phenomenologically, as we do today when we say, "the sun sets.")[23]

Galileo could have avoided controversy regarding the Earth's movement by handling his book, *The Dialogue,* in a different way.[24] The church prohibited him from believing in a moving Earth or defending it, but he

---

21. See Hannam, "Mythical Conflict," paras. 1–8, 17–32.
22. Hannam, "Mythical Conflict," paras. 9–14.
23. See Hannam, *Genesis of Science*, 310, 320–22.
24. See Galileo, *Dialogue.*

could discuss it and teach it (and so could everyone else) as a *hypothetical*. That is, he could teach it as: "*If* the Earth moved around the sun, these are the calculations that would describe it." Instead of doing this and then describing the opposite view objectively as he could have, Galileo foolishly took the Pope's beliefs and put them in the mouth of *Simplicio*, the intellectually hapless character in the book. The Pope was understandably furious, even though he was friends with Galileo. Galileo's insult at the end of the book practically forced the Pope to act, for political reasons. Unfortunately for Galileo, this meant having him arrested.[25]

However, when he was arrested and brought to the Inquisition, Galileo was not put in prison, but was put under house arrest in the prosecutor's apartment, an immaculate six-bedroom abode complete with a servant. After eighteen days of interrogations, he was moved to the *Villa Medici* in Rome, a palace owned by the grand duke of Tuscany. He may have been able to avoid prison because he was a celebrity of his day, and he did have a (stormy) relationship with the Pope, as well as the protection of the Medici family. There is absolutely no evidence that he was ever actually thrown in prison.[26]

It has likewise been assumed for 250 years that Galileo had been tortured, based on the documents that the Pope released about Galileo at the time. But it turns out there is no evidence that he was tortured. As Ronald Numbers explains, there is "no doubt that Galileo was threatened with torture during the June 21 interrogation. But there is no evidence that he was actually tortured, or that his accusers planned actually to torture him. Apparently, the 'rigorous examination' mentioned in the sentence [released to the public] meant interrogation with the *threat* of torture, not interrogation under actual torture."[27] In fact, Numbers goes on to say: "Inquisition authorities in Rome rarely practiced torture, further reducing the likelihood that Galileo experienced this punishment. Inquisitorial rules exempted old or sick people (along with children and pregnant women) from torture, and Galileo was not only elderly but suffering from arthritis and a hernia."[28] Thus, it's highly unlikely that Galileo was harmed.

Of course, what was done to Galileo was still horrible. It is never right to force someone to change their political, religious, or theological beliefs.

---

25. Hannam, *Genesis of Science*, 325, 331–32.
26. See Numbers, *Galileo Goes to Jail*, ch. 8, "Myth 8."
27. Numbers, *Galileo Goes to Jail*, ch. 8, "Myth 8," (emphasis mine).
28. Numbers, *Galileo Goes to Jail*, ch. 8, "Myth 8."

But the point is that most of our beliefs about what happened to Galileo are inaccurate.

After the trial, Galileo was returned to his home under house arrest and remained under house arrest until his death in 1642. But his arrest still allowed him to write another brilliant book, *Discourses on Two New Sciences*, which was smuggled out of Italy and published in the Netherlands.[29] The truth is that Galileo was a celebrity. After his discoveries with his telescope in 1611, when he went to Rome he was given "a hero's welcome," even though the meaning of his discoveries was still being debated.[30] And when *The Dialogue* was published in 1632, it was extremely popular. In sum, Galileo was neither imprisoned nor tortured, and his censure was rather cushy. He continued to be very influential despite the Inquisition.

THE INQUISITION IN THE MIDDLE AGES

> DR. BARRON: Without guidance, [the Mintakan] religion could degenerate into inquisitions, holy wars, chaos.

This mention of the Inquisition from Dr. Barron occurs during his debate with Captain Picard about how best to mitigate the cultural contamination on the planet. Would the Mintakan religion degenerate into "inquisitions?"

What was the Inquisition in the Middle Ages really like?[31] Well, it was made up of independent priests in different parts of Europe, who would investigate people (mainly theologians) when it was thought they were teaching false theological ideas. For the most part, it wasn't a centralized operation run by the Pope but was localized and much less powerful than commonly thought. Medieval universities investigated their own students and teachers, and it was very rare for inquisitors to get involved in these investigations. In such settings, when a student turned in a thesis that contained heretical beliefs, he was simply allowed to make "corrections" to his paper, usually with no punishment and no harm to his reputation.[32] Regarding inquisitors, when they convicted someone of heresy, the convicted person was rarely punished physically. Instead, the person was often

---

29. Hannam, *Genesis of Science*, 334.
30. Hannam, *Genesis of Science*, 319.
31. See Hannam, "Frequently Asked Questions," paras. 2–3, 7.
32. Hannam, "Science and Church," paras. 17–23; and Hannam, "Frequently Asked Questions," para. 7.

required to go on a pilgrimage. Most of the time, punishments were rather mild. One estimate using records of the Spanish Inquisition showed that roughly 1.4 percent of the cases resulted in execution, a small percentage.[33] Of course, the Inquisition was a brutal and terrible thing. It's just that common stereotypes of it are often inaccurate.

A FLAT EARTH?

There are a host of other myths believed today that support the "Dark Ages" idea. For example, it's often thought that people in the Middle Ages believed the Earth was flat, and that Columbus was warned about going on his expedition because if he sailed too far, he would fall off the edge of the Earth. This is completely false, on a number of levels.[34]

First, it is simply not the case that people believed the Earth was flat in Columbus' day, or even earlier in the Middle Ages. One of the first calculations of the Earth's circumference was by an ancient Greek scholar, Eratosthenes (died 294 BC). He appears to have come up with a circumference of roughly 23,000 miles, just shy of the 24,900-mile actual circumference. Pliny the Elder, a Latin writer, took Eratosthenes' figure and promoted it. In Columbus' day, Pliny was the popular scholar to cite, so Eratosthenes' figure was generally accepted. Scientists in Columbus' day were not warning him about a flat Earth, but that he underestimated the size of the Earth, thus underestimating how long it would take to sail to the East Indies. His plans for the trip were rejected on these grounds.

We now know that these scientists were correct. Columbus' figures were much too small. If he hadn't blundered into the Americas, it's likely he and his sailors would have died of starvation on the open ocean. Where did we get the idea that Columbus triumphed over a flat Earth? It appears to have originated with Washington Irving (died 1859), who wrote a novel on Columbus in the nineteenth century and invented the idea that people in the Middle Ages believed the Earth was flat.[35]

What about the church being anti-scientific during the Middle Ages? This is also completely false, in that natural philosophers, the precursors to today's scientists, were all church leaders. They were the ones who were making discoveries about nature and disseminating that information.

33. Hannam, "Frequently Asked Questions," paras. 9, 16.
34. See Hannam, "Myth of the Flat Earth," paras. 1–7.
35. Hannam, "Myth of the Flat Earth," para. 6.

Dark Ages or Enlightenment?

Priests and leaders such as Rector John Buridan (c.1300–1361), Bishop Nicole Oresme (c.1325–1382) and Albert of Saxony (c.1316–1390) speculated on the solar system, what a vacuum was actually like, and brought mathematics to bear on their ruminations about the world. Not to mention the fact that European universities arose in the twelfth century and produced most of the brightest minds that led to (pre)scientific discoveries. Even in the twelfth century, universities were autonomous corporations which allowed for creative intellectual thought.[36]

In short, most of what is believed about the Middle Ages today is wrong. So when Picard characterizes the "Dark Ages" as being full of "superstition and ignorance," he is spectacularly uninformed. It seems clear that he is simply following Gene Roddenberry's ideas here, which, as we have seen, are not based on solid historical evidence.

"I don't look down on people who believe [in religion]," Roddenberry once said, "any more than I would scorn a child's need for Santa Claus."[37] He then went on to explain:

> As the human race moves into adolescence and adulthood, it can no longer afford to guide its affairs via those simple myths. Our human ancestors thought long and hard on who and what they were and came up with the best explanations they could make. The frightening thing is that we—almost at the end of the twentieth century, entering the space age, becoming a society based on knowledge—are still hanging on to those explanations, which date back to our Stone Age. I think we need a more fruitful way to analyze these questions . . . I don't dislike religion, but I am in considerable fear of what today's brand of it can lead to.[38]

Here we see Roddenberry's belief that religious ideas are mythical, ancient, and superstitious, exactly the attitude Picard had in the conference room. As we've seen, these assumptions are unmistakably false, at least when it comes to the history of the Christian Middle Ages on Earth. In the next chapter we'll see more of Roddenberry's humanist beliefs in "Who Mourns for Adonais?" (TOS).

---

36. Hannam, *Genesis of Science*, 66–68, 177–92.
37. O'Quinn, "Inside Gene Roddenberry's Head," 19.
38. O'Quinn, "Inside Gene Roddenberry's Head," 19.

5

Petty Gods and Noble Humanity

"Who Mourns for Adonais?"
(*The Original Series*)

WATCH "WHO MOURNS FOR ADONAIS?" (TOS SEASON 2)

IN THIS EPISODE, A being of great power who claims to be the Greek god Apollo accosts the *Enterprise* and demands worship from the crew. Holding the *Enterprise* in place with a giant forcefield that looks like a hand, Apollo threatens the crew with destruction if they refuse to worship him, forcing Kirk and a few of his crew to beam down to Apollo's planet. Kind one moment and wrathful the next, Apollo has the ability to punish the crew with lightning from his fingers and other feats if they don't give him the worship that is "rightfully his." But a defiant Kirk isn't fooled for a minute and refuses to worship Apollo. A power struggle ensues. When Apollo is attracted to Lt. Carolyn Palamas, Mr. Scott's love interest in the episode, Scotty attacks, but is knocked out cold with a wave of Apollo's hand. Apollo then leaves with Carolyn. He explains to her that gods need adoration and worship, or they die.

Kirk theorizes that perhaps thousands of years ago, space travelers visited Earth, their great power mistaken for the supernatural, making them the basis for the Greek myths. Kirk's only hope is to make Apollo angry by refusing to worship him, and then to attack him while he is in a weak state after he's expended energy with his "miraculous" displays. His forcefield continues to hold the *Enterprise* in place.

On Kirk's orders, Carolyn spurns Apollo's love. Furious with her, Apollo grows into a giant four stories high. With a mighty wind, he overshadows Carolyn, who is helplessly thrown to the ground. On board the *Enterprise*, Spock determines a method for piercing Apollo's forcefield. He fires phasers on the Olympian edifice where Apollo's throne sits, which is the source of Apollo's "miraculous" power. The phasers disintegrate the building in spite of Apollo's screams to stop. His divine abilities destroyed, a distraught Apollo cries out to Hera and the other Greek gods, disappearing into the wind, never to return.

WORLDVIEW ANALYSIS

> KIRK: If you want to play god and call yourself Apollo, that's your business, but you're no god to us, Mister.
>
> APOLLO: I said you will worship me!
>
> KIRK: And you've got a lot to learn!

In this episode we again see clear humanist beliefs and assumptions, especially in the way that the crew reacts to Apollo. It's not just that the crew is skeptical of Apollo's claim to be a god. It's that they never consider, even for a moment, he could be divine in any way. When Chekov says, "I've never met a god before," and Kirk responds, "And you haven't yet," it's clear there is no *possibility* in the crew's minds that Apollo could be anything other than an alien. Whatever powers Apollo has, there is no explanation other than a purely material, scientific one.

It makes sense, of course, to get tricorder readings on Apollo to see what kind of being he really is. But even if he had been pure energy, or another sort of energy that the crew had never encountered before, they still would have assumed he was an alien and not a god. The question is, is there anything McCoy's tricorder *could have* registered that would have convinced them they were dealing with a god? It appears not. But why assume gods don't exist? The Federation has only explored a tiny fraction of the galaxy. How do they know divine beings don't exist somewhere?

Interestingly, the *Enterprise*'s reaction to Apollo is contrary to the attitudes of the crew on *Deep Space Nine* when encountering the Prophets

SECTION II: HUMANISM IN *TREK*

and their enemies, the Pah-Wraiths. In an episode called "The Reckoning," even though the Prophets and the Pah-Wraiths registered as energy beings on the station, Captain Sisko and his crew knew they were supernatural entities and treated them as such. It took time for Sisko to realize that the Prophets were more than aliens—they were divine beings who could predict the future. But by the end of the series the religious nature of the Pah-Wraiths and the Prophets was clear.

> KIRK [TO CAROLYN]: We're human. We couldn't escape from each other even if we wanted to. [We're] a bit of flesh and blood afloat in a universe without end. The only thing that's truly yours is the rest of humanity.

Kirk's humanist assumptions are clear as he speaks to Lt. Palamas about betraying Apollo. He assumes there is no God and that the material universe is all there is and all there ever will be. This means that the only thing we have as human beings is each other. As we've seen, Roddenberry often put these humanist beliefs, near and dear to his heart, into *Star Trek*.

> APOLLO: You have made me proud. Now you can rest . . . We shall remember together. We shall drink the sacramental wine . . .
>
> McCOY: May I ask what you offer in exchange for this worship?
>
> APOLLO: Life in paradise. As simple and as pleasureful as it was those thousands of years ago on that planet so far away.

In these snippets of dialogue, Apollo is using Judeo-Christian language. The biblical language of "rest" is likely related to Sabbath observances, and "wine" is related to the sacrament of communion. In communion, participants eat bread and drink wine to commemorate Jesus' death for our sins. As well, it is likely that when Apollo refers to "paradise," he is referencing the garden of Eden in the book of Genesis. Greek mythology had a paradise, called the Elysian Fields, but it referred to the afterlife, not a place where people could flourish before they died. Of course, the gods had to send a person to the Elysian Fields after death, and Apollo certainly claims the power to give people paradise here in the episode.[1]

However, when Apollo says, "I would have loved you as a father loves his children," he echoes biblical terminology which sees God the Father as the first person of the Trinity, and us as his children. Ps 103 says: "As a father has compassion on his children, so the Lord has compassion on those

---

1. See Greenberg, "Elysian Fields," paras. 1–2, 7–17.

who fear him; for ... he remembers that we are dust" (Ps 103:13–14). This theme is repeated in the New Testament: "To all who received him [Jesus], to those who believed in his name, he gave the right to become children of God..." (John 1:12).

By using Christian terminology, Roddenberry tips his hand that he is commenting on the Judeo-Christian God, embodied in the character of Apollo. But Apollo's character is not flattering, and neither is Roddenberry's view of the Judeo-Christian God.

IS THE GOD OF THE BIBLE VENGEFUL AND ANGRY?

> McCOY: You saw how capricious he is. Benevolent one minute, angry the next. One more wrong move from [Carolyn] and he could kill her.

Apollo's insecure demands for worship, his need to feast on praise in order to survive, and his capricious threats to vengefully destroy the Enterprise crew if they don't cooperate, match many of Roddenberry's views of the God of the Bible.

At a *Star Trek* convention in the 1970s, for example, Roddenberry revealed his opinions of the biblical God in a tongue-in-cheek monologue about network censors and the Bible. Would the networks allow several risqué scenes from the Bible to run on network television? Roddenberry thought not. He then said that God's wrathful outbursts in the Bible were so violent, they were too bloody for network television. God's character was so petty that his "constant demands for praise" indicated a "personality insecurity."[2]

Is Roddenberry right? Is God vengeful, unpredictable, and insecure like Apollo?

The Bible says God is "compassionate and gracious, slow to anger, abounding in love" (Ps 103:8). His love is self-sacrificial, its ultimate demonstration in the sacrifice of his son to save the world from sin. In the New Testament, the Greek word *agape* describes God's radically generous and unconditional love which sacrifices for the good of the other, putting the needs of the other ahead of the needs of self. The sacrifice of his son for us exemplifies what true love really is (Rom 5:6–8, 1 John 4:9–10).

---

2. Roddenberry, "Letter from a Network Censor."

But in this episode, we don't see this kind of unconditional love from Apollo. Apollo is simply using the *Enterprise* crew to get something he desperately needs—worship. His love is *conditional*—he will love them *if* they give him what he wants. Hence, the crew is simply a means to an end, and when they don't cooperate, Apollo punishes them with his wrath. His insecurity leads to his angry outbursts.

Is the God of the Bible like this? Does he lose his temper because he's insecure or surprised? According to Christian theology, God is never insecure because he is perfectly sovereign over all the universe. Therefore, nothing is outside his sovereign will. For example, Job 42:4 says, "I know that you can do all things, and that no purpose of yours can be thwarted." Prov 19:21 says, "Many are the plans in the mind of a man, but it is the purpose of the Lord that will stand." And Ps 103:19 declares, "The Lord has established his throne in the heavens, and his kingdom rules over all." Finally, Eph 1:11 states that we have been "predestined according to the purpose of him who works all things according to the counsel of his will." These are just a sample of many verses that declare God rules over all, and nothing is outside of his control. (Although when we say "control," we do not mean God is the immediate cause of every action in the universe, which would make him responsible for sin. We only mean that everything done is either caused or allowed by his will. Things he allows are not necessarily condoned, but necessary if he is to allow sentient beings to have free will.)[3]

It follows then, that when the Bible says God "becomes angry," he is not insecure about something out of his control that he must reign in. His wrath is not a response to environmental stimulus.

As well, if God's anger is part of a "personality insecurity," then he would be reacting in surprise to something. But according to Scripture, unlike pagan gods, God knows all, including the future, so nothing can surprise him. His omniscience is declared in a few, and implied in many verses of Scripture. For example, Ps 147:5 says, "Great is our Lord, and abundant in power; his understanding is beyond measure." And in Ps 139, David says:

> O Lord, you have searched me and known me!
> You know when I sit down and when I rise up;
>   you discern my thoughts from afar.

---

3. For a discussion of the logical compatibility of free will and predestination, see ch. 6. For an academic defense of the logical compatibility of a perfectly good God and evil, see Plantinga, *God, Freedom, and Evil*. For a popular summary of such arguments see Craig and Moreland, *Philosophical Foundations*, 540–55.

> You search out my path and my lying down
> and are acquainted with all my ways.
> Even before a word is on my tongue,
> behold, O Lord, you know it altogether. (Ps 139:1–4 ESV)

Here David says that God knows his thoughts, he knows what David will say before David says it, and that there is nowhere David can go from his presence. This implies omniscience. First John 3:20 says God is "greater than our hearts, and he knows everything." Many other verses imply God's omniscience (Ps 44:21, 147:4, 1 Kgs 8:39, 1 Chr 28:9, Isa 40:28, Matt 10:30, Acts 1:24, Heb 4:13). Given God's omniscience, then, God's wrath is not a reaction. God cannot be surprised by anything because he knows all, including the future.

For the reasons stated above, theologians dating back to the first centuries of Christianity have seen most biblical verses referencing God's wrath as anthropomorphic, as well as anthropo*pathic*. They are anthropomorphic in that they ascribe human attributes and reactions to God which are analogous to our attributes, but not the *same* as ours. And they are anthropo*pathic* in that they ascribe human emotions to God that are, again, similar to what humans have but different in crucial respects.[4] God feels anger, but it is not human anger which reacts in surprise or insecurity and then overtakes his reason. Rather, his wrath is a consistent, rational displeasure at anything that contradicts his holiness or destroys us, his precious children. In other words, his anger is not an out-of-control emotion, instead it is always in line with his reason. Because he is perfectly rational, an emotion is never the *reason* for his wrath (although it may accompany it). Instead, rational reasons, in perfect alignment with the facts, are the basis for his wrath. Therefore, his anger is a *response* to his reason, not the other way around as it is for us.[5]

This conclusion is supported by the multiple uses of the term "wrath" in Scripture. According to Kinghorn and Travis in their book *But What About God's Wrath?*, language about God's wrath in which it "breaks out" on people (2 Sam 6:8), is "poured out" on people (Ps 79:6, Jer 42:8, Ezek 36:18), or "comes on" or "falls on" people (Num 1:53, 18:5, 2 Chr 19:2, Zeph 2:2), is talking about a "pattern of action" on God's part. The language used implies something that God has thought out, rather than simply a reaction to a stimulus. As well, Isa 59:18 says that God's wrath "settles accounts"

---

4. See Lane, "Wrath of God," 145.
5. See Kinghorn and Travis, *What About God's Wrath?*, 20–22.

against people, again implying rational deliberation. While it is true that our anger is "not always appropriate," God's anger is always appropriate because it is based on his (infallible) reason.[6]

When we arrive at the New Testament, Paul equates God's wrath not with an emotion, but with the natural consequences of sinning against him. In Rom 1, Paul says, "the wrath of God is being revealed from heaven," and when people sinned, God *"gave them over* in the sinful desires of their hearts"* (Rom 1:18, 24). "Gave them over" indicates that, as a considered judgment, God allows the natural consequences of sin to catch up to us whenever we indulge in it.

Hence, God's wrath is not simply an emotion. It also includes his decisions of judgment which include either his actions carrying out these decisions, or his decision to allow natural consequences to take place and thus punish those who sin. When God feels anger, it includes his carefully deliberated actions, meaning he has *reasons* for his wrath. This supports the conclusions above that since God is omniscient and sovereign over creation, his anger is simply not like ours. As Kinghorn and Travis put it, "there is an important distinction between anger *accompanying* an action and anger *motivating* an action." Anger motivates us, but not so with God.[7]

IS GOD'S ANGER SELF-CENTERED, LIKE APOLLO'S?

> APOLLO: Agamemnon was one such as you, and Hercules. Pride and arrogance. They defied me until they felt my wrath . . .
>
> KIRK: I have four hundred and thirty people on that ship up there.
>
> APOLLO: No, you do not, Captain. They are mine. To save, to cherish, or to destroy at my will.

Is God's anger self-centered? We need to understand that when we say God's anger "burns against" anything that is against his holy nature, this does not refer to a selfish, human emotion. Since God is perfectly holy, it is impossible for him to *not* be against anything that is unholy.

What does it mean to say God is "holy"? It is a rich term in Scripture, but for our purposes here, God's "holiness" simply means he never chooses to do evil, nor is he tempted by evil. Rather, he *always* chooses the good. He

---

6. See Kinghorn and Travis, *What About God's Wrath?*, 13, 19–21.
7. Kinghorn and Travis, *What About God's Wrath?*, 21.

is perfectly righteous, and since his righteousness is perfect, it is impossible for him *not* to be against anything that is unholy.

Thus, rather than a selfish emotion, God's opposition to unholiness is simply the rational outworking of his perfect and unchanging holy nature. To put it another way, it is God's nature to *always* oppose unholiness wherever it is found, and to support holiness wherever it is found, whether that holiness is in his own nature, in us, or something else. It is simply what his nature requires. It is not a selfish, emotional response.

We must also remember that God created *us* for holiness, intending for us to always choose the good. He created us originally as righteous beings, and we wrecked our original nature when we sinned. When we continue to act in an unholy way today, we further damage our original human nature, which was simply not created to accommodate unholiness. Thus, God's opposition to unholiness includes his fatherly love to protect us from self-destruction.

WHAT ABOUT GOD'S JEALOUSY?

Biblically, God's appropriate anger is also part of his *love* for us, and it is similar to a marriage relationship. In Exodus, the Israelites commit only to God. When God says he is a "jealous" God (Exod 20:4–6), it is because he has made us for *him alone*: "For your Maker is your husband—the Lord Almighty is his name" (Isa 54:5). In Exod 24, the Israelites take part in a ceremony that commits themselves only to him, much like a marriage ceremony. Later, when they worship other gods, it is analogous to adultery.[8]

This is similar to human love in an important way. If a husband confesses to his wife that he's had an affair, anger on her part is the proper response. It is "appropriate anger" because her husband has committed *only* to her. He belongs to her exclusively, and he has broken his promise. If she reacts with indifference, we would conclude that something was wrong with their marriage in the first place, that in fact, she didn't love her husband.

We then see that the Bible compares God's jealousy at times to a cheated lover. For example, Ps 78:57–58, speaking of Israel, says, "Like their fathers they were disloyal and faithless . . . They angered him with their high places; they aroused jealousy with their idols." ("High places" are hills upon which the Israelites worshipped idols, which sometimes included child

---

8. See Lamb, *Emotions of God*, 72–75.

sacrifice and religious prostitution.)[9] And Hosea, again speaking of Israel, says, "Rebuke your mother [Israel], rebuke her, for she is not my wife, and I am not her husband. Let her remove that adulterous look from her face..." (Hos 2:2). This is some of the strongest language in the Bible that indicates God wants an intimate relationship with us. He is to be as close as a spouse is to us, and we should commit to him only. (In Scripture, a healthy marriage is a reflection of God's relationship with us—although not a *worship* relationship. See for example, Eph 5:25–32 and Rev 19:7–9.) Thus, when we worship something other than God, he is appropriately jealous (and appropriately angry).

In summary then, we see that while God's righteous anger responds to unholiness, it is not like our anger in that it is never an out-of-control response to something that has surprised him or made him feel insecure. Instead, it is his reasoned, fully deliberated response to anything that is unholy, which is why many descriptions of God's anger in the Bible are simply anthropomorphic. His anger is not like ours.

DOES THE GOD OF THE BIBLE NEED WORSHIP?

> APOLLO: I want from you that which is rightfully mine. Your loyalty, your tribute, and your worship... A god cannot survive as a memory. We need love, admiration, worship, as you need food.

Apollo uses force to demand worship from Kirk and crew because he *needs* praise. And he believes worship is due him simply because he is more powerful than the *Enterprise* crew. Is the God of the Bible similar to Apollo? Does he desperately need worship?

The short answer to these questions is no. For one thing, God doesn't demand praise because he needs it. The Bible says he needs absolutely nothing. In the Old Testament, God differentiates himself from pagan gods by declaring that he does not need sacrifices or worship:

> I will not accept a bull from your house or goats from your folds. For every beast of the forest is mine, the cattle on a thousand hills ... all that moves in the field is mine. If I were hungry, I would not tell you, for the world and its fullness are mine. Do I eat the flesh of bulls or drink the blood of goats? (Ps 50:9–12 ESV)

---

9. Bible Gateway, "High Place," paras. 1–4.

Here the tone is ironic and comic. God is satirizing pagan gods by asking, in effect, "Am I a weak and hungry God, waiting desperately for the next sacrifice to fill my belly?"[10] God owns all the animals on the planet, and he does not need sacrifices.

As well, if God needed worship like we need food, he would not be self-existing. But the Bible indicates he is eternal, which means he is self-existent. In Psalm 102 it says:

> Of old you founded the earth,
>   and the heavens are the work of your hands.
> Even they will perish, but you endure;
>   And all of them will wear out like a garment;
> Like clothing you will change them and they pass away.
> But you are the same, and your years will not come to an end.
> (Ps 102:25–27 NAS)

Thus, God has no need that, if it were not met, he would cease to exist. He is self-existent because he is eternal. He does not need worship or anything else.

Why then does God command worship? For two reasons. First, because *we* need it. God created us with souls that need to worship, and this explains why, when God is not recognized by a culture, the culture fabricates its own gods to venerate. As Augustine famously said:

> And so we ... who are a due part of your creation, long to praise you ... You arouse us so that praising you may bring us joy, because you have made us and drawn us to yourself, and our heart is restless until it rests in you.[11]

Second, God commands worship because it is rational to do, and he is a rational being. That is, worship of God is perfectly fitting because God is perfectly good, perfectly powerful, perfectly loving, and perfectly knowledgeable. In these ways he is completely different from Apollo.

In Christian theology, God is the supreme Good in the universe, and all goodness in the world is a dim reflection of his. Thus, God commands us to worship him because it is entirely rational to do so, and all his commands are the rational outworking of his holiness. He is not commanding us to worship him out of selfish motives, nor is he demanding worship simply because he is more powerful than us. We worship him because it is rational

---

10. Craigle, *Psalm 1–50*, 366.
11. Augustine, "Our Heart Is Restless," paras. 1–2.

to worship the ultimate good in the universe, and God happens to be that Good.

Jonathan Edwards recognized God as the foundation of all goodness in the universe in his essay, "The Nature of True Virtue":

> God is not only infinitely greater and more excellent than all other being, but He is . . . the foundation and fountain of all being and all beauty; from whom all is perfectly derived, and on whom all is most absolutely and perfectly dependent . . . [His] being and beauty is . . . the sum and comprehension of all existence and excellence.[12]

Given he is the ultimate Good in the universe then, we are entirely rational to worship him alone. In fact, Rom 12:1 says, "Therefore, brothers and sisters, I urge you, in view of God's mercy, to offer your bodies as living sacrifices, holy and pleasing to God—this is your spiritual act of worship." But "spiritual" here is *logikos*, which is related to logic. There is much debate about this term, but it can be translated "reasonable" or "logical" here. That is, it is fitting and reasonable to worship God because of his goodness and mercy toward us.[13]

WERE ANCIENT GODS VISITORS FROM OUTER SPACE?

> KIRK: Apollo's no god. But he could have been taken for one once . . . Say five thousand years ago, a highly sophisticated group of space travelers landed on Earth around the Mediterranean.

This concept is similar to the theme in "Who Watches the Watchers" (see chapter 4), except here Kirk theorizes that ancient gods like the Greek gods or the Egyptian gods were supposedly visitors from outer space.

These ideas gained popularity in the 1960s with their publication in the French magazine *Planete,* which translated and disseminated ideas about aliens from H.P. Lovecraft, a horror writer from the 1920s and 1930s.[14] In 1968 Erich von Däniken took these ideas and fashioned them into the international bestseller *Chariots of the Gods*, published a few months after the

---

12. Edwards, "Dissertation," para. 2.

13. See Moo, *Romans*, 753. Moo defines *logikos* as more than "reasonable" or "logical," but the idea is included.

14. Colavito, "Charioteer of the Gods," paras. 4–5, 11.

airing of "Adonais." According to *Skeptic Magazine*, von Däniken wrote his bestseller by plagiarizing ideas from Lovecraft and the book *Morning of the Magicians*, written by *Planete* editors Louis Pauwels and Jacques Bergier.[15] In his book, von Däniken suggests that only alien visitations can explain certain discoveries like the Egyptian Pyramids, and that certain Mayan inscriptions appear to reveal aliens from other planets.

But modern archaeologists have summarily dismissed these claims as pseudoscience. For example, von Däniken claims that Egyptians didn't have the technology to build the pyramids, so aliens must have been involved. But tomb paintings depict how huge two-and-a-half-ton stones were moved with ropes, wooden sledges, and ramps into place. And Egyptians had the tools to cut and polish the soft limestone used.[16] In fact, we now have an ancient papyrus which logs the transportation of limestones most likely used to build the pyramids.[17] Contrary to von Däniken's claim that the choice of location for the Great Pyramid was a "mystery," it was clearly a location that could hold the six-million-ton pyramid, and it was close to the limestone used to build it.[18]

As well, von Däniken's claim that there is an "ancient astronaut" on a Mayan sarcophagus lid is dismissed by archaeologists who know the engraving as "Pakal, the central figure, falling backward into the jaws of the underworld." One of von Däniken's claims, that stone giants of a similar style can be found at Easter Island and Tiahuanaco, in Bolivia, can be discredited by simply comparing photographs of the two stone statues. Another critique of von Däniken's book indicates that some of its claims can be cleared up simply by visiting the Peruvian Gallery at the Penn Museum![19] Von Däniken is clearly not an archaeologist, and he made simple mistakes archaeologists would not make. There is no evidence that ancient astronauts have visited Earth, either to be worshipped by humans or for any other reason.

When Kirk declares, "Most mythology has its basis in fact," he seems to be referring to this idea of alien visitations. Importantly, his conclusion that gods sometimes grow tired is based on his idea of alien visitations—an

---

15. Colavito, "Charioteer of the Gods," paras. 2–10.
16. Legrand and Boese, "Chariots of the Gods?," 365–66.
17. Klein, "Egypt's Oldest Papyri," paras. 1–2.
18. Legrand and Boese, "Chariots of the Gods?," 365–66.
19. For these and other critiques of *Chariots of the Gods?* see Epstein, "Scholars Will Call It Nonsense."

idea for which he offers no evidence. He then uses the (unsubstantiated) conclusion that gods sometimes grow weary to defeat Apollo.

> KIRK: Mankind has no need for gods. We find the one quite adequate ... We've outgrown you. You asked for something we can no longer give.

These are further statements about how humans have outgrown their need for gods. But according to Kraemer, Cassidy, and Schwartz, the line "we find the one quite adequate" is "more likely to be one of the creator's [Roddenberry's] throwaway lines designed to mollify American viewers than a serious indication of Kirk's offended or outraged monotheistic beliefs."[20] At any rate, as we saw in the last chapter, the idea that scientific progress has eradicated religious belief is fallacious. As science has progressed in the United States, religious belief among scientists has stubbornly persisted, as it has in the population at large.[21] There is no reason to think that in the twenty-third century, even with advanced Starfleet technology, religious beliefs would disappear. And in many *Trek* episodes and series, they *don't* disappear.

---

20. Kraemer et al., *Religions of Star Trek*, 25, 5–6.
21. See ch. 4 on "Who Watches the Watchers." See also Ecklund, *Science vs Religion*.

SECTION III

Christianity in *Trek*

INTRODUCTION

As we saw in chapter 2, Gene Roddenberry put Christian themes and symbolism in *Star Trek* from the very beginning. Although he didn't consider himself a Christian, he wanted to placate audiences, the networks, and the censors. Amazingly, in pitching *Star Trek* to different networks in 1964, he included a possible story about an alien who resembles Jesus undergoing crucifixion on another planet. As we will see, there are many Christian ideas sprinkled throughout *Trek*, including the latest series from Paramount+.

In this section, we examine fascinating Christian themes in different *Trek* episodes, from an exploration of predestination and free will in "Children of the Comet" (SNW) to a surprise Christian ending in "Bread and Circuses" (TOS). We'll also discuss more on how advanced technology is interpreted by religious believers in "New Eden" (DIS). And don't miss volume 2, where we will discuss more *Trek* episodes about Christianity.

As you watch the episodes in this section, pay careful attention to what they say about Christian beliefs and worldview. Does a philosophy of peace and brotherhood affirm Christian beliefs as a whole, or merely some of its ethical imperatives? Does Christianity require pacifism, or does it allow for self-defense? As well, if God predestines something to come about, does that mean we cannot freely choose the future? How do predestination and free will go together? As we'll see, the episodes in this section raise a number of fascinating philosophical and religious questions.

6

Free Will or Fate?
"Children of the Comet" (*Strange New Worlds*)

WATCH "CHILDREN OF THE COMET" (SNW SEASON 1)

IN THIS EPISODE, CAPTAIN Pike and the crew of the USS *Enterprise* discover a comet headed toward a planet with a developing culture that does not have the technology to know it is in danger. Pike decides to divert the comet so it will not destroy the planet and kill millions of its inhabitants. But as the *Enterprise* fires photon torpedoes to divert the comet, they discover it has a shield. Cadet Uhura, Lieutenant Spock, and a landing party beam down to the comet to see if they can lower the shield. They find an interior cave on the comet that has clearly been designed by a culture with advanced technology. It has a gigantic egg-shaped energy source at the center of it.

Meanwhile, the *Enterprise* is fired upon by an alien ship, piloted by beings who call themselves "The Shepherds." They warn the *Enterprise* not to interfere with the comet, which they call M'hanit, claiming it is "an ancient arbiter of life." When Pike informs them that the comet is on a trajectory to hit the planet and kill millions, the Shepherd commander is adamant: "If it is [M'hanit's] will to move, he will move. If it is his will to bring life, he will bring life. If M'hanit wills the planet to die, even chooses to die with it . . . it is preordained." Neither the Shepherds nor the *Enterprise* are allowed to interfere, even though millions will perish.

SECTION III: CHRISTIANITY IN *TREK*

On the comet, the landing party finds they are trapped inside the room with the egg, and Uhura has to translate its markings so they can leave the room and beam back up to the ship. She discovers the alien language responds to music and harmonics. One of the melodies she randomly tries opens the egg and lowers the shields on the comet, which means they can beam out.

Unfortunately, the Shepherds are aware of the landing party, and calling it "sacrilege," they begin firing their superior weapons on the *Enterprise*. Taking evasive maneuvers, the *Enterprise* finds a way to divert the comet without actually touching it. Spock launches in a shuttle, and moving in behind the comet, radiates heat from his shields. Traveling down the right side of the comet, his shields warm the ice in the comet and shear off a section of its mass. The comet misses the planet. But because of water vapor melting off the comet's close flyby, rain begins to fall on the planet, turning it from a desert waste into a luscious world perfect for agriculture. Pike wonders, "So, did it actually 'bring life?'"

Later, Pike is stunned by Uhura's report of the language from the comet. The deciphered message she received from the comet predicted it would miss the planet, but she received the message *before* Spock diverted the comet. This means the comet knew Spock would divert it beforehand. The *Enterprise*'s intervention was taken into account by the comet's ancient, predestinated path. The mollified Shepherd commander tells Pike, "You have seen the glory and the mercy that is M'hanit. Perhaps in the future you . . . will not judge the faith of others."

WORLDVIEW ANALYSIS

In this episode we have a fascinating lesson on fate and the theological idea of predestination. When something is preordained, is it actually possible to change the outcome? Or does preordination mean the future is impossible to change regardless of whatever free-will decisions we make, including decisions to avoid the predicted outcome?

> UNA: Chris, have you considered that maybe your fate isn't written? . . . What if your fate is what you make it?

This episode is bookended by discussions between Captain Pike and Una, the first officer. In the previous episode, Pike had a vision of how he will be made an invalid ten years in the future, when he is severely injured saving several crew members from death. We, of course, know that this will occur because in the TOS episode "The Menagerie," Pike is utterly paralyzed, and can only communicate using one beep for "yes" and two for "no." *Strange New Worlds* takes place chronologically before "The Menagerie." In SNW, we have now discovered how and why Pike's accident occurred. But Una tries to encourage Pike that, even though he has seen the vision, it is not written in stone. Perhaps it's malleable. There may be a way to save the crewmembers and save Pike from destruction as well. "Your fate is what you make it," she tells him.

But the message of this episode is the opposite, as we see with the diversion of the comet and its own knowledge of the future.

> PIKE: You're suggesting the comet had foreknowledge of future events?
>
> UHURA: The comet's flight path and its . . . mission to seed that planet was predicated on [Spock] flying that shuttle to move it. It knew its fate . . .

In this last scene we discover that the message Uhura had received before the comet was diverted means that the comet knew it wouldn't hit the planet. But Uhura was only able to translate the message after Spock had diverted the comet. This means that the comet's foreknowledge took into account the free decisions of the *Enterprise* crew. It knew it would be diverted by Spock and bring life to the planet before the event occurred.

WHAT IS PREDESTINATION?

The word "preordained" is an old term used in Christian theology to describe God's predetermination of what will happen in the future. In today's Bible translations, it's usually called "predestined" or "chosen," and people who are chosen are called "the elect." For example, Eph 1:4–5 says:

> For he *chose* us in him before the creation of the world to be holy and blameless in his sight. In love he *predestined* us for adoption to sonship through Jesus Christ, in accordance with his pleasure and will . . .

In other words, God chose Christians to know him before he created the world and adopted us "as his sons." This latter phrase is a translation of a Greek word meaning legal adoption of male heirs in Roman culture, but it applies to both men and women here.¹ God chose us according to his "pleasure," which means he was *delighted* to choose us.² The idea that we are chosen fits well with 1 John 4:19, which says, "We love because he first loved us." According to Christian theology, it was God who made the first move toward us, to love us and adopt us.

The Bible also indicates that broader events and history are foreordained. For example, Dan 2:20–21 says, "Praise be to the name of God for ever and ever; wisdom and power are his. He changes times and seasons; he deposes kings and raises up others. He gives wisdom to the wise and knowledge to the discerning." And Isa 14:24–26 says, "The Lord Almighty has sworn, 'Surely, as I have planned, so it will be, and as I have purposed, so it will happen . . . This is the plan determined for the whole world; this is the hand stretched out over all nations.'"³

HOW DO PREDESTINATION AND FREE WILL GO TOGETHER?

The verses above raise a number of questions. First, if God predestines something, is it possible to bring about a different future? Another way to ask this is, if the future is known in advance (whether through God or some other means), is it possible to change the future? The famous Greek tragedy *Oedipus Rex* offers a fascinating take on the answer. Oedipus' parents receive a prediction that he will grow up to murder his father and marry his mother. In spite of their strenuous efforts to avoid this future, it comes about anyway. In several twists of fate, Oedipus ends up unknowingly killing his actual father and marrying his mother by mistake. Oedipus' fate was inevitable, regardless of the decisions he or his parents made to avoid it. Since the future was known, it was impossible to change.

In Christian theology, we ask such questions like this: If God determines what happens in the future, how are we held accountable for our actions? Would that make him the author of evil? If he chooses some people to know him, what about those he does not choose? How is it fair that he chooses some and not others? How do we have free will if the future is determined?

1. Hoehner, *Ephesians*, 196–97.
2. Hoehner, *Ephesians*, 198–99.
3. The context here is God's plan to defeat the Assyrians in Israel, but the principles of God's foreordination apply broadly.

In order to understand the answers, we need to take a dive into Christian philosophy and a theory Christian philosophers have proposed called middle knowledge, or Molinism. It was first proposed by Luis de Molina, a sixteenth-century monk, and independently discovered in the 1970s by Alvin Plantinga, a philosopher best known for his work at Notre Dame. The theory proposes that God knows alternate pasts and alternate futures.[4]

Middle knowledge fits well with 1 Sam 23:6–13, which describes David's flight from Saul as Saul tries to kill him. David plans to hide in a town called Keliah, but he hears Saul is coming to Keliah to possibly destroy it if he hides there. So David asks God, "Will the citizens of Keliah surrender me to him? Will Saul come down, as your servant has heard? . . . The Lord said, 'He will'" (1 Sam 23:11). So David left Keliah and didn't stay there. This means that when God said, "he will," God wasn't speaking of the actual future but an alternate future. *If* David hid there, Saul *would* come, and the citizens *would* hand him over. But since David left Keliah, Saul didn't actually arrive there.

Middle knowledge proposes that God knows alternate pasts and alternate futures, including the free decisions people make and how those affect the future. He knows all propositions in the subjunctive tense, such as, "If David were to hide in Keliah, the people of the town would give him up to Saul." God knows these propositions as part of his omniscience, his knowledge of everything that is logically possible to know. Thus, he arranges events in history, knowing how people would freely choose, given certain circumstances that could occur. And he either brings about or allows those circumstances to occur. Thus, he knows how people will freely choose and what will happen in the future as a result.

Does this mean that because God brings about certain circumstances, we are forced to choose a certain way? No, according to the model our decisions are free decisions. The circumstances are not the *immediate causes* of our decisions, but merely part of the *end purposes* for them.[5] For example, if I am driving east on Marlatt Avenue, the immediate cause of my car heading east is my pressure on the gas pedal, which causes a chain of events, including combustion, that propels the car eastward. But what is the end purpose of my driving? The end purpose is that because I am hungry, I

---

4. For philosophical defenses of middle knowledge, see Molina, *On Divine Foreknowledge*, 46–61; and Plantinga, *Nature of Necessity*, 169–80.

5. See Falcon, "Aristotle on Causality," sect. "2. The Four Causes." An "immediate cause" is what Aristotle calls the "efficient cause," the cause which brings about change. An "end purpose" is Aristotle's "final cause."

want to eat lunch at a Mexican restaurant on the east side of town. The end purpose is the reason for which I choose, not the immediate cause of the event. According to middle knowledge, the circumstances in which I choose provide the end purposes for my decisions, not the immediate causes. The hunger I feel does not cause me to go to the restaurant, because of course, I can refuse to eat. Instead, my hunger is part of the circumstance that motivates me to freely choose to go to the restaurant. My decision is not merely a domino that falls because of the dominos that fall before it. This means that God can bring about or allow circumstances to occur and know what I *would* choose given those circumstances, but I still freely make my choices. Since he brings about those circumstances, he knows what will actually occur.

Note that middle knowledge is one *possible* way God could bring about the future he wants to occur. Since it is a logically possible way, it solves the *logical* problem of how free will and predestination go together. To solve the logical problem of predestination and free will, we do not need to know how God actually brings about the future, but merely one logically possible way he could do it.

Thus, middle knowledge explains the logical problem of how God could predestine us to enter a relationship with him, but we still freely choose him. On a middle knowledge view, God's predestination of those who are chosen simply means that he brings about (or allows) the circumstances under which he knows that such persons would freely choose him. But since they choose for end purposes (and not immediate causes), they freely choose God in the circumstances he brings about. Thus, *he* chooses us to be adopted as his children, but *we* still freely choose him.

But if God created a good world knowing evil would come about, how is he not responsible for the evil in it? Part of the answer is that in order for God to make a world in which we freely choose him, we had to have the ability to choose evil. If he did not give us this ability, then we couldn't love him, because love requires free choice; it cannot be forced. If I were to pull a gun on someone and say, "Tell me you love me," when they say they love me it would not be real love. God cannot make a world in which we are forced to freely choose him, because that is a logical contradiction, like a square circle. God cannot make "forced love" or square circles because such things are logical contradictions and cannot exist. And the laws of logic cannot be anything other than what they are. They are an unchanging part of God's perfect, exhaustive knowledge. Thus, God's omnipotence, the fact that he's all-powerful, means that he can create everything that is *logically possible* to create. He cannot create "forced love."

Therefore, since God wanted a world in which we freely choose to love him, he created the possibility of evil in our world. But the possibility of evil is not the same thing as creating evil. When I go snow skiing, there is the possibility of serious injury or death. But the risk is still worth the enjoyment of skiing. Skiing is *good*. This raises another question.

WHY COULDN'T GOD CREATE A WORLD IN WHICH HE ENSURES EVERY PERSON FREELY CHOOSES HIM?

If God is all-powerful, why couldn't he create such a world? Well, given that he has already decided he wants to uphold our free will, suppose it is the case that for some people to freely choose God, others might have to freely reject him. The circumstances under which a person might freely choose God could include the decisions of others who freely choose to reject God. For example, a brother who rebels against God and experiences the consequences of his decision might be part of the motivation for his sister to freely accept God.[6] Like the movie *Back to the Future*, just one decision in the past that Marty's father made completely changed Marty's future, because that one decision had ripple effects for numerous other decisions made afterward.[7] Someone's decision against God could have ripple effects for a person years or centuries later who freely chooses him. As part of God's omniscience, he simply knows every one of these combinations. While he could perhaps create a world with only a few people in it to ensure they would all freely choose him, he preferred a world populated by numerous people, on this view.

Further, it is possible that since God has middle knowledge, he could arrange the history of the world such that for the maximum number of people who freely choose to be in a relationship with him, there is a minimum number of people who would reject him. It is even possible that God arranges history so that, for every person who freely chooses against God, there was *no possible world in which they would have freely chosen him*. That is, in every possible world God could create, they would freely reject him. So, on this view, the number of people in this world who reject God are people who would never have chosen him anyway, in any possible

6. For this discussion, see Craig, *Only Wise God*, 145–51.
7. Strobel, *Case for Faith*, 186–87.

circumstance that could exist. Since this is logically *possible*, it solves the logical problem of the fairness of why God would choose some people to be in relationship with him and not others. Those who are not chosen would never have freely chosen him in any possible world God could create.[8]

Thus, middle knowledge allows us to understand one possible way God could know ahead of time that a comet would not strike a planet but seed it instead, based on the free decisions of the *Enterprise* crew to divert the comet. God knows the comet will miss the planet because he knows what the ship's crew would choose, given the circumstances that he allowed to come about.

SCIENTIFIC BACKGROUND OF THE EPISODE

> UNA: The sublimation is nudging the comet off course.
>
> PIKE: And for the record, we're not actually touching it.

Part of what it means to critically analyze a story includes comparing what happens in it with what we know of real science. The problem with the script here is that the "sublimation" of the comet cannot actually alter the course of the comet, because sublimation simply refers to the process of the comet's ice changing directly from a solid to a gas, without going through the liquid state (which happens because of the cold vacuum of space). The sublimation, and the comet's tail, have nothing to do with the propulsion or direction of the comet.[9] However, if watched closely, Spock's shuttle, with its heat shields on maximum, creates sublimation that is shearing off a section of the comet on its right side. Changing the mass of the comet would change its direction, and that appears to be the intent of the script.[10] Simply warming the ice with heat shields will do nothing to change its course, unless the mass of the comet changes, and it does change here. The script doesn't explain this process, which makes for a confusing scene.

> SPOCK: If we are correct and the comet communicates through music, it would be logical to assume that it is speaking to us right now.

---

8. Craig, *Only Wise God*, 148–50.

9. ThePlanetsToday, "Sublimation and Comet Tails," paras. 1–5.

10. If the comet lost mass its vector would change. See Gregerson, "Conservation of Linear Momentum," para. 1. For the intent of the script here, see Stobie, "Recap—Children of the Comet," para. 6.

Free Will or Fate?

[UHURA sings].

UNA: The comet's force field just disappeared.

Here, Uhura happens to find the harmonics that lower the comet's shields in just a few minutes of musical guessing. Since she doesn't know the comet's language and is studying it for the first time, it's highly unlikely that it would take her only a few minutes to lower the shields. It could take weeks, even months, to decipher the language and hit on precisely the correct notes. For comparison, watch the sci-fi epic *Arrival*, in which it takes a linguist, played by Amy Adams, weeks, if not months, to decode the aliens' language since it has never been encountered before. The idea that Uhura could do it in a matter of hours borders on incredulity.

PIKE: Who hit us?

ORTEGAS: Uh, they did.

As well, there is the problem of how the Shepherds' ship surprised the *Enterprise*. Their ship fired on the *Enterprise* at close range, and the question is, why didn't the *Enterprise*'s sensors pick it up light years away? Constitution-class starships like the *Enterprise* have the ability to pick up such ships on their sensors from great distances. There is no explanation that the Shepherds' ship had a cloaking device such as the Romulans use, or any other similar technology. Again, *Strange New Worlds* needs help in the science department.[11]

SHEPHERD COMMANDER: You have seen the glory and the mercy that is M'hanit . . . Perhaps in the future, you will not be so quick to judge the faith of others.

What a delightful ending, in that we see that the people who had faith, the Shepherds, were right all along. They knew that, whether the comet struck the planet or didn't, what came about was "preordained." And they were right.

This is a fascinating story about predestination and free will. The fact that the comet "knew" it would be diverted by Spock ahead of time hints at the ways God can know the future, even though what happens in it is based on the free decisions of people he has made. Pike and his crew learn an important lesson about fate and faith here. But the scientific basis for the script is mixed and confusing at best.

11. The show *does* have a science advisor. See Flatow and Macdonald, "Star Trek's Science Advisor," paras. 1–3.

7

Is Faith Always Blind?

"New Eden" (*Discovery*)

WATCH "NEW EDEN" (DIS SEASON 2)

THE USS *DISCOVERY*, CAPTAINED by Christopher Pike, is investigating seven red "signal bursts" that have appeared across Federation space. The crew follows a red burst to a planet at the outer reaches of the galaxy, where they find genuine human inhabitants in a pre-warp society. Pike and Burnham debate what the red signal bursts mean. Could they be from an intelligence, or even from a divine source? Pike quotes Clarke's third law: "Any sufficiently advanced extraterrestrial intelligence is indistinguishable from God." But Burnham chides Pike for thinking that there may be a reason for the signal bursts besides a scientific explanation.

Since the settlement on the planet is a pre-warp society, the Prime Directive applies, and the *Discovery* crew cannot tell the people there of their technology, nor can they critique the settlers' faith.

The crew beams down to the settlement where they explore a church that has symbols from all of Earth's major religions, including Christianity, in its stained glass windows. There is a sacred text with fire-and-brimstone warnings for those who do not believe, and one of the stained glass windows appears to have a picture of a red angel.

The inhabitants of the town tell of a red angel who appeared on Earth during the nuclear war two hundred years ago, and saved the people who were taking refuge in a church from a huge explosion that would have killed them all. The angel transplanted them to their current planet with the church intact, and they have been worshipping the Red Angel ever since. Burnham is determined to figure out a scientific explanation for how the inhabitants got to the planet, since, she reasons, it can't have been a real angel. But the spiritual leader of the group says, "We have no need of proof. We are guided by the existence of something greater . . . our faith."

Meanwhile, the *Discovery* finds that there is a gravitational problem with the outer ring of the planet, and some large radioactive particles are breaking free from the ring and headed toward the planet. The radiation will cause an "extinction-level event." This seems to be the reason the red signal burst brought the *Discovery* to the planet. The crew is able to divert the particles, saving the inhabitants.

Back on the surface, Jacob, one of the inhabitants, thinks he knows that Pike and his crew are from Earth and that they came on a starship. He tells them he has a soldier's helmet from the time their ancestors were saved by the Red Angel, with video on it about what happened. But he has no power source to watch the video.

In the end, Pike decides the Prime Directive is worth setting aside to gain the access they need to the video so they can learn more about the Red Angel. He tells Jacob the truth about who they are in exchange for the helmet. When he and Burnham watch the helmet video, they see the same Red Angel who brought the inhabitants to the planet, saving them two hundred years earlier. The angel looks very much like the one that appeared to Burnham when she was injured on an asteroid during their last mission.

At the end of the season, we learn that the Red Angel is a time travel suit worn by Gabrielle Burnham, Burnham's mother, and Burnham herself, from the *future*. The future Michael Burnham used the suit to travel to the past and alert the *Discovery* to places in the galaxy where the timeline needed to be corrected. Thus, the Red Angel was not a real (supernatural) angel after all.

WORLDVIEW ANALYSIS

With "New Eden," we see some old themes about technology and the miraculous. But we also see new themes about how faith and reason go together, and about major religions having common beliefs.

SECTION III: CHRISTIANITY IN *TREK*

BURNHAM: This [stained glass] is two centuries old. It represents not just Christianity, but Judaism, Islam, Hinduism, Buddhism, Shinto and Wicca.

Here we see a church that supports many of the world's different religions. Is the episode making a positive statement about religion, even though Commander Burnham and Captain Pike are skeptical of the inhabitants' religious beliefs? Discussing the episode, Producer Alex Kurtzman is enigmatic on the question: "In the original series, religion doesn't exist. Yet, faith is something that has always been a major topic in different ways. The idea of this mystery [the Red Angel] that has no answer immediately suggests a presence or force greater than anything anyone has ever known. It was intriguing to us."[1]

WHAT IS OMNISM? IS IT A RATIONAL WORLDVIEW?

When Pike and crew beam down to the planet and explore the church there, they observe one of the stained glass windows, which has symbols from seven Earth religions on it. And there is a sacred text cobbled together from different world religions. The stained glass design is similar to symbols for omnism, the belief that all major religions have common wisdom, and that no religion is superior to others or has absolute truth. In other words, all religions have common rules and ethics, and (often) all refer to the same higher power (although omnists can be agnostic as well). There are a wide variety of beliefs in omnism.[2] Is omnism a rational worldview, and thus possibly true?

Many of the world's major religions do have very similar ethical beliefs, such as the golden rule: "Do unto others as you would have them do unto you" (Luke 6:31). Most religions have rules about lying, stealing, murder, and other basic ethical commands. As well, most religions believe in some kind of higher power that is worth knowing. So, it *is* true that all, or most, religions share some similar wisdom.[3]

The problem is that for most religions, the ethical systems and beliefs in a higher power are just part of a larger whole, and many of the most important beliefs in world religions contradict each other. Christianity,

---

1. See Bloom, "'Star Trek' Showrunner," para. 14.
2. See Luzong, "Omnism 101," paras. 4–10.
3. For a thorough comparison of the world's major religions, see Smith, *World's Religions*.

Judaism, and Islam believe in one God, while Hindus believe in many, and different forms of Buddhism differ on whether gods exist at all. When it comes to Jesus, Christians believe he died on the cross and rose again to save the world from sin. Muslims believe Jesus was a prophet, but most believe he wasn't crucified, killed, or risen. Instead, he was translated to heaven without dying. They don't believe Jesus is God, and neither do followers of Judaism, who believe Jesus was merely an ethical teacher.

There are two problems with omnism. First, one must take a very shallow view of the world's major religions to believe they are compatible, or that they teach, on the whole, the same wisdom. Belief in one God is essential to some religions and not others, and of course, Jesus' death and resurrection for sin is central to Christianity, but not to other religions. Since these major religions disagree on such central beliefs, it's impossible to take them all seriously and believe they teach largely the same ideas. Though most (not all) have similar ethical standards and believe in some sort of spirituality, such beliefs are only a part of what makes these religions what they are.

Remember in the introduction we saw how using logic and critical thinking was crucial for understanding what is true. The most fundamental law of logic is the law of noncontradiction. Two statements cannot both be true if they contradict each other in the same way and at the same time. Hence, there is either one God or there is not. Either Jesus' death paid the penalty for the sins of the world, or it did not. It is impossible to believe that there is one God and there is not at the same time. Thus, the only way to affirm all the world's major religions is to jettison most of their central beliefs, and to only focus on their ethics and a vague belief in a higher power. But, with Christianity, for example, one cannot know God except through Jesus, and this is central to its belief system. Thus, the idea in omnism that there is similar wisdom in all the world's religions is somewhat trivial, given that there is so much central to these religions that is mutually contradictory. There are too many contradictions in the *central* beliefs of the world's major religions for them all to be true. Thus, to say each world religion is "legitimate" because they all have a "fragment of truth" is nonsensical.[4] In what sense are they "legitimate" if so many of their beliefs are false?

Second, to believe all religions have a "fragment of truth," one must believe that the world's religions all have part of the truth of a larger whole, much like the Hindu parable of the blind men touching an elephant: One

---

4. These quotes are from Luzong, "Omnism 101," para. 5.

blind man touches the trunk and says, "an elephant is like a snake." Another blind man touches a leg and says, "an elephant is like a tree," and a third touches the side of the elephant and says, "an elephant is like a wall." They are all correct because they are touching a different part of the elephant. But, how does the omnist know this is the case? To claim that each religion believes a part of a larger whole, the omnist must maintain a privileged position: that, while other religious believers are blind, seeing only part of the whole, the omnist is *not* blind, and can see the whole elephant. While the omnist claims no religion has "absolute truth," he believes in an absolute truth himself: that each religion only sees part of the larger whole. How does the omnist know that this is the case? It appears omnism is simply based on an emotional desire not to "judge" other religions. This, of course, is fine to believe as long as there is evidence for such a belief.

> PIKE: The original purpose of a window like this [was] to teach the gospel to those who couldn't read . . .
>
> ALL-MOTHER: Peace be with you.
>
> PIKE: And also with you.

With "teach the gospel," and "peace be with you," we see Christian terminology used by both Pike and the All-Mother, the spiritual leader of the settlers. The religious language she uses, and her title as "All-Mother" *do* reflect a combination of different world religions. Yet the use of the phrases above gives her religious beliefs a Christian tint and sets us up for a commentary on Christianity in the episode.

IS FAITH AN IRRATIONAL LEAP IN THE DARK?

> ALL-MOTHER: We have no need of proof. We are guided by the existence of something greater than ourselves—our faith.

Here the All-Mother mentions a common belief held about faith today: that if you have evidence for your beliefs, faith is superfluous. On this view, faith is believing things that cannot be proved, or for which there is no evidence.

If faith is believing in something with no evidence, does this mean it is an "irrational leap"? Should we use faith, rather than reason, to pursue religious truth?

Is Faith Always Blind?

The view that we must have faith despite, or apart from the evidence, is known as fideism. Fideism is often traced to Soren Kierkegaard, a Christian philosopher in the nineteenth century. Here it is important to delineate between aspects of Kierkegaardian thought that are fideistic and those that are not.

Kierkegaard is famous for teaching that faith is offensive to reason, a belief "by virtue of the absurd." He points to Abraham's test of faith in which God tested him by commanding him to sacrifice his son Isaac (Gen 22:1–19). God had already promised Abraham that he would make him into a great nation through Isaac and his offspring (Gen 12:1–3, 15:1–6, 18:1–15). Now he was commanding Abraham to sacrifice his son. Since child sacrifice is wrong, Abraham had to suspend his faith in human reason and take a leap in the dark, trusting that even though God commanded him to kill Isaac, he would get Isaac back *in this life*. Thus, Abraham had to suspend his trust in the "ethical," to radically trust in God. But did this mean Abraham wasn't using reason at all?

When Kierkegaard says that Abraham believed "by virtue of the absurd," and that faith is "offensive to reason," he was saying that, according to Abraham's human understanding, God's promise and his command contradicted each other, and that God asked Abraham to do something that appeared to be immoral. But Abraham *reasoned* that, since God is good, and he is all-powerful, he would somehow work this out, and it would not be immoral for Abraham to do. He already knew God's voice, as he had heard it many times before. He knew it was God speaking, and he knew God is good. While it was beyond his power to work out the dilemma, *God* would work it out.[5] Heb 11:19 says, Abraham "reasoned" or "was convinced," that God could raise Isaac from the dead. The Greek word for "reasoned" here is *logizomai*, which can be translated "reasoned" or "an inward conviction or persuasion."[6] The Angel of the Lord stopped Abraham at the last second from sacrificing Isaac, and thus, "in a manner of speaking, [Abraham] did receive Isaac back from the dead" (Heb 11:19). Thus, Abraham was not jettisoning *all* reason, he simply used a higher form of reason. Although what God asked him to do was "at the limits of human understanding," he reasoned that "for God, everything is possible." He believed "by virtue of the absurd," but this was "never a logical impossibility," but was "always in

---

5. Mark Bernier, in discussion with the author, May 25, 2023. See his *Task of Hope in Kierkegaard*, 186–209, especially 188.

6. O'Brien, *Letter to the Hebrews*, 410, 434.

reference to what is 'humanly impossible.'"[7] That is, Abraham believed God could do things humans could not. Therefore, Abraham wasn't believing in a logical contradiction (which *would* be irrational), but only something that God, in his wisdom, knew that Abraham did not. This is a critical distinction. Abraham was not believing that God could take logically contradictory statements and make them consistent (statements such as: "I must kill Isaac, but he will be made into a great nation," or "God is moral, but he is commanding me to perform child sacrifice"). Abraham just believed that since God is all-powerful, he could raise Isaac from the dead, or he would work it out another way. And this is what happened. God worked it out by stopping Abraham at the last second from making the sacrifice. This is a relational type of faith that says, "I know God, and I know he's good. I know this is beyond my understanding, but he will work it out for my good in the end." And he did. In this sense, Kierkegaard is not a fideist.

On the other hand, Kierkegaard *did* believe that doctrines such as the Trinity and the incarnation were "paradoxical" (regarding the Trinity: How could one God be three persons? on the incarnation: How could Jesus be fully God and fully human at the same time?). Since these doctrines are an affront to reason, the believer must make a "leap" beyond human reason to believe them, according to Kierkegaard. Thus, he has no use for classical arguments for God's existence, the resurrection, the logical coherence of the Trinity, and so forth. Here Kierkegaard goes too far in his belief in the paradoxes of Christian doctrine, and he *is* a fideist at this point, since he says the use of reason in believing such doctrines is superfluous. While Christians would not know of such doctrines apart from God revealing them (through the Bible or through the Holy Spirit, for example), arguments for God's existence, the logical coherence of the Trinity and the incarnation, etc.,[8] can be immensely helpful in opening up intellectual space for someone who is considering becoming a Christian.

---

7. Bernier, *Task of Hope in Kierkegaard*, 188, 191.

8. For defenses of the logical coherence of the Trinity, see Swinburne, *Christian God*, 170–91; and Davis et al., *The Trinity*. For a defense of the logical coherence of the incarnation, see Morris, *Logic of God Incarnate*. For an overview of arguments for God's existence, see Craig and Moreland, *Philosophical Foundations*, 475–509.

HOW DO FAITH AND REASON GO TOGETHER?

What can be said, then, about the relationship between faith and reason? Martin Luther made a helpful distinction in his theology between the "magisterial" and the "ministerial" use of reason. He said in the "magisterial" use of reason, Christians use reason over and above God's revelation (in Scripture) to judge whether it is true, using evidence and argument to make that determination. In the "ministerial" use of reason, Christians submit their reason to God's revelation and the gospel. Given that the Holy Spirit convicts the believer that Christianity is true (John 16:8), reason supplements the Spirit's witness, rather than supersedes it.[9] This fits with Anselm's view of "faith seeking understanding." Our "active love of God seeks a deeper knowledge of God."[10]

What does this mean for apologetics, the rational defense of the Christian faith? In the classical view of apologetics, believers *know* Christianity is true through the Spirit, but they *show* Christianity is true through reason.[11] It is the testimony of the Spirit which grounds the Christian's faith.[12] Rom 8:16 says, "The Spirit himself testifies with our spirit that we are God's children." And Jesus said, "the Advocate, the Holy Spirit, whom the Father will send in my name, will teach you all things and will remind you of everything I have said to you" (John 14:26).[13]

But the believer demonstrates Christianity is true through reason, just as Paul the Apostle did when he testified about Christianity on his missionary journeys. In Acts 17, for example, it says:

> As was his custom, Paul went into the synagogue, and on three Sabbath days he *reasoned* with them from the Scriptures, explaining and proving that the Messiah had to suffer and rise from the dead. "This Jesus I am proclaiming to you is the Messiah," he said. (Acts 17:2–3)

The word Greek for "reason" here is *dialegomai*, which means, "reason," "argue," "dispute," or "discourse." In other words, Paul was building a case, or

---

9. See Craig, *Reasonable Faith*, 47–48. Alvin Plantinga offers a philosophical defense of the idea that the Holy Spirit convicts people of the truth of Christianity in his *Warranted Christian Belief*, 241–323.

10. Williams, "Anselm," paras. 5–6.

11. Craig, "Classical Apologetics," 28–45.

12. See note 9 above.

13. See also John 14:16–17, 20–21, 1 John 2:20, 26–27, 3:24, 4:13, 5:6–10.

an argument, much as a lawyer would, that the Messiah described in the Old Testament is Jesus, and that Jesus had to die and rise from the dead.[14]

Thus, we can see that when the All-Mother says "We have no need of proof," but we have "faith," she is offering a fideistic view of faith that is not supported by Scripture. While it may seem irrational to trust God when one cannot see how he will bring something about, it actually *is* rational to trust him, since he is all-powerful and all-knowing. He can know what we do not, and he has the power to bring about circumstances that we cannot. However, it is *not* rational to blindly believe in doctrines like the Trinity or the incarnation when at the same time we believe they are logically contradictory. They cannot be contradictory and also be true.

THE RED ANGEL

> PIKE: Why did that second signal want us to come here?
>
> BURNHAM: As science officer, I would advise restraint in ascribing motivation to what are now simply unidentifiable energy bursts.
>
> PIKE: "There are more things in heaven and earth, Horatio . . ."
>
> BURNHAM: I know my Shakespeare, Captain. Are you suggesting that some kind of divine intervention put those people on the planet?
>
> PIKE: I assume you're familiar with Clarke's third law? "Any sufficiently advanced extraterrestrial intelligence is indistinguishable from God." I have no idea how or why they're here, but I highly doubt it's by accident.
>
> BURNHAM: Certainly a bold interpretation, sir.

Here Pike wonders why the signal burst led them to the planet, and Burnham chides him for being unscientific. When he quotes Hamlet, "There are more things in heaven and earth," he is referring to supernatural explanations, since the context of Hamlet's statement is the appearance of Hamlet's father as a ghost (which Horatio can't bring himself to believe). Burnham rightly realizes Pike is talking about supernatural appearances and she pushes back. It's unscientific to believe in anything but a physical explanation.

---

14. See also the use of *dialegomai* in Acts 18:4, 19, 19:8–9, 24:12, 25, Mark 9:34, Heb 12:5, and Jude 9.

Is Faith Always Blind?

We have already discussed Clarke's third law (and Michael Shermer's modification, which Pike quotes here) in chapter 4. Recall that, even though advanced technology might appear to be magic at first, "primitive" people quickly learn how to adapt to and acquire such technology for their own uses. And in "New Eden," we see Jacob stubbornly believing that Pike and his crew are from a starship and travel to other planets. This is partly because this idea has been handed down to him by his forebears, but clearly, the inhabitants of the planet are sophisticated enough to see that humans could have advanced technology that would appear supernatural.

This scene also cleverly trades on an ambiguity regarding the word "intelligence" in Pike's quote of Clarke's law. With the Hamlet quote and the fact that Pike tells Burnham the structure is a church, Pike appears to be referring to the supernatural. But when he quotes Clarke's third law and says "I highly doubt it's by accident," he *could* be referring to the supernatural, but he could also be referring to an extraterrestrial intelligence that is mistaken for the divine. The latter idea foreshadows what we actually learn at the end of the season: that indeed the Red Angel *was* an intelligence which lured the *Discovery* to certain locations in the galaxy to avert disasters and save innocent people. Pike and Burnham were both right. There was an intelligence, and it wasn't by accident. But it wasn't supernatural. It was Michael Burnham herself, traveling from the future wearing the Red Angel suit, bringing the *Discovery* to locations across the galaxy to fix the timeline.

VIOLATING THE PRIME DIRECTIVE

> PIKE [SPEAKING OF JACOB]: Look, I feel for the guy, too. But even angels are no excuse for violating General Order 1.
>
> BURNHAM: Yeah, well, I have a better excuse. His helmet camera.

In this scene, Burnham convinces Pike to violate the Prime Directive so they can get access to the soldier's helmet that Jacob has, which contains video of the Red Angel when it saved the settlers. Pike returns to the church basement and tells Jacob what he always wanted to know: that the real Earth is still there, technologically advanced, and people can travel between the stars. "I know what it's like to have doubts," Pike says, and Jacob replies: "My entire family spent their whole lives hoping to get a confirmation that what we believed was true."

SECTION III: CHRISTIANITY IN *TREK*

There are two interesting aspects of this scene. First, the discussion of faith and doubt isn't about faith in a higher power, but a secular faith that the Earth has survived nuclear war and become technologically advanced. It's a twist on the traditional "faith vs. doubt" conundrum, which usually has to do with faith in organized religion (see chapter 3).

Second, Pike and Burnham break the Prime Directive here to get the helmet video. If it really is true, as we saw in chapter 4, that a captain should sacrifice his entire crew not to violate the Prime Directive, it comes across as unfathomable here that Pike just sidesteps it with so little debate or discussion. Since *Strange New Worlds* takes place only a decade or so before *The Original Series*, it's entirely implausible on the part of the writers of this episode to wave away the Prime Directive so easily. No doubt Gene Roddenberry (an excellent writer in his own right) is rolling over in his grave.

8

The Son Rises on Rome
"Bread and Circuses" (*The Original Series*)

WATCH "BREAD AND CIRCUSES" (TOS SEASON 2)

In "Bread and Circuses," the *Enterprise* explores the last known position of the Federation ship SS *Beagle* and traces the debris of the vessel to a planet that appears to have a Roman Empire, very similar to Earth's but with twentieth-century technology. The *Beagle* was commanded by an old friend of Captain Kirk's, R.M. Merik. Kirk, Spock, and McCoy beam down to investigate. The Prime Directive applies since the planet has a pre-warp culture.

Kirk and crew are captured by several men and taken to a hidden settlement of former slaves who worship the sun and believe in a brotherhood of peace. The former slaves have foresworn violence. Flavius, formerly a famous gladiator in the games, tells them he "heard the words of the sun. Words of peace and freedom," and he no longer fights. "There is one true belief," he says.

Flavius agrees to escort Kirk, Spock, and McCoy to the city to find Merik, who is now known as "Merikus," and is head of the Empire. They are captured by Roman soldiers and taken prisoner to be thrown into the games, which are televised live across the Empire. The three men are allowed to see Merikus and his second in command, Claudius, who invite

SECTION III: CHRISTIANITY IN *TREK*

them to a lavish meal but tell Kirk he must order all his crew down to the planet to permanently join Roman society, just as Merik has done. The strongest crewmembers will survive Roman barbarism, and the weak ones will be killed in the arena. Kirk refuses, so they put Spock and McCoy into the arena and force Kirk to watch his friends fight to the death against Roman gladiators. Spock is able to knock out his opponent, and performs the Vulcan nerve pinch on McCoy's opponent, rendering him unconscious. With the games thwarted, Spock and McCoy are then taken back to their cells, while Kirk contemplates their fate and whether he will beam down his crew to save them. When he refuses, his execution is scheduled for the arena the next day. The night before, he is left alone in Claudius' quarters and attended to by Claudius' female slave, whom Kirk sleeps with that night. Claudius tells Kirk he wanted to give him one last night "as a man."

The next day Kirk is brought to the arena for a "simple execution." But on board the *Enterprise*, Scotty finds a way to shut down the electricity in the city just as Kirk is to be killed. He, Spock, and McCoy are saved and beamed back to the ship right before they are run through with Roman swords.

Back on the *Enterprise*, Spock remains puzzled about one aspect of their Roman society: How could sun worship, a primitive religion, have produced a "brotherhood of peace"? Lt. Uhura tells them they have it all wrong. The inhabitants aren't worshipping the sun, but the Son of God. Another Roman society will be superseded by Christianity. "Wouldn't it be something to watch? . . . To see it happen all over again?" Kirk muses.

WORLDVIEW ANALYSIS

> UHURA: I've been monitoring some of their old-style radio waves, the Empire spokesman trying to ridicule their religion. But he couldn't. Don't you understand? It's not the sun up in the sky. It's the Son of God.
>
> KIRK: Caesar and Christ. They had them both. And the word is spreading only now.
>
> McCOY: A philosophy of total love and total brotherhood . . .

While some of the lines in "Bread and Circuses" are somewhat "sentimental" and "preachy," as Marc Cushman puts it, they are nevertheless fascinating.[1] Note that the Roman leadership in the story "couldn't ridicule" the Christian religion, as it was evidently too profound. And note Kirk's willingness to embrace the "total brotherhood" of the Christians on the planet. He tells Flavius to go right on believing it. Altogether, this episode contains an encouragingly positive take on Christianity.

But as Robert Asa points out, the admiration of Christians in the show is about the Christian *ethic*, the philosophy of love. It's not an embrace of Christian beliefs per se, but the ethical result they produce.[2] In other words, the worshippers of the Son only describe Christian morality, not any Christian doctrines, such as doctrines of the Trinity, the incarnation, etc. As we have already seen, Roddenberry thought such doctrines were "nonsense."[3] So Roddenberry's focus here on the core of Christianity is love, brotherhood, and pacifism.

DOES CHRISTIANITY REQUIRE PACIFISM?

KIRK: Then you heard the word of the sun?

FLAVIUS: Yes. The words of peace and freedom. It wasn't easy for me to believe. I was trained to fight. But the words, the words are true.

In this story, the Christians are pacifists and refuse to fight in the games because they are against violence. The words of "peace and freedom" captured Flavius' imagination, and he gave up fighting in the arena. (Yet we see how he struggled with his commitments and defended himself when he was tossed back into the games.) It appears as if the "words of the Son" prohibited violence of any kind.

Should Christians renounce violence and follow a pacifist lifestyle? Since there are godly Christian thinkers on both sides of this issue, we should always graciously disagree with others. So, how should we think about this?

Pacifism certainly fits with the first few centuries of Christianity. The first Christians were persecuted both by Jewish religious leaders and various Roman authorities, and they did not fight back. Jesus famously said:

---

1. Cushman, *Voyages: TOS Season Two*, 331.
2. Asa, "Classic Star Trek," 46–47.
3. See ch. 2.

Section III: Christianity in *Trek*

> You have heard that it was said, "Eye for eye, and tooth for tooth." But I tell you, *do not resist an evil person*. If someone strikes you on the right cheek, turn to them the other also. And if anyone wants to sue you and take your shirt, hand over your coat as well. If anyone forces you to go one mile, go with them two miles. Give to the one who asks you, and do not turn away from the one who wants to borrow from you. (Matt 5:38–41, emphasis mine)

Here Jesus says clearly, "Do not resist an evil person . . . Turn the other cheek." On the face of it, this certainly appears to teach pacifism, especially because he gives no exceptions here as he does to his injunctions in other places. (For example, Jesus prohibits divorce but allows for an exception in Matt 5:31–32.)

There is also the issue of leaving judgment to the Lord. We are never to take revenge on someone who has done evil because God will punish evildoers in the end, and his perfect punishment will always be proportional to the crime. Therefore, we do not take on the task of punishment ourselves. Paul says in Rom 12:

> Do not repay anyone evil for evil. Be careful to do what is right in the eyes of everyone. If it is possible, as far as it depends on you, live at peace with everyone. Do not take revenge, my dear friends, but leave room for God's wrath . . . "If your enemy is hungry, feed him; if he is thirsty, give him something to drink. In doing this, you will heap burning coals on his head." Do not be overcome by evil, but overcome evil with good. (Rom 12:17–21)

This passage seems to reinforce Jesus' teaching that we should not resist evil people, but let God judge them in the end. God will judge everyone who does evil, and in Revelation, Jesus comes to judge evildoers at the end of the age.[4] At the very least, the verses above seem to teach, on an individual level, to love our enemies and not resist them. The violence we inflict in self-defense would thus be "repaying evil for evil," and, at least at first glance, not allowed.

Augustine of Hippo (AD 354–430) is considered the father of modern just war theory. He endorses these passages as requiring a nonviolent response *in certain cases*. He believes we are required to respond nonviolently when we can see that a peaceful response would teach the offender spiritual truths, such as that our worldly goods are not our own and our

---

4. For a summary of these pacifist arguments, see Southon, "Defense of Christian Pacifism." See also Hauerwas, "Pacifism," 277–83.

heavenly home is more important than this earthly one. "The right time for this [nonviolent response] to be done is when it seems likely to benefit the one for whose sake it is done, in order to bring about correction and return to agreement," he says.[5] Thus, as Langan points out, Augustine does not absolutize a nonviolent response in every case but sees it as *instrumental*. A pacifistic response is required when it can do the offender some good. The patience of the victim can "convert the mind and heart" of the offender.[6] Whether we embrace Augustine's view of a pacifistic response in certain cases, or we believe it is required in every case, this is impossible to do in our own power. We can only love our enemies in the power of the Holy Spirit.

When we combine theological arguments with the destructiveness of modern warfare, we can also buttress a case for pacifism. Thanks to modern technology, we now have the capability of wiping out whole cities with nuclear weapons. But we also have the capability to bomb distant buildings and soldiers in faraway countries with drones that are piloted remotely from installations here in the U.S. And even before the U.S. dropped two atomic bombs on Japan in World War II, we and other nations were carpet-bombing cities, using bombers to lay waste and set fire to entire cities, killing hundreds of thousands of civilians.[7] With the ancient invention of the cannon, the capability of causing large explosions and killing multiple soldiers simultaneously was achieved. And since the invention of the repeating rifle, we have the capability of killing multiple people with bullets in a matter of seconds, especially with today's automatic weapons. This, of course, was not true of earlier warfare, in which fighting was hand-to-hand, and combatants (often) followed what were considered virtuous rules of combat. Today we can destroy huge amounts of property and people with one touch of a button from great distances away. Because of this, and the fact that people who lose their lives in a war are irretrievably lost, (and any time a person's life is taken it is gone forever),[8] war is a great evil, and should be avoided if at all possible.

In some famous cases, courageous pacifistic resistance has been effective. In Denmark during the Nazi occupation in World War II, Danish

---

5. Langan, "Elements of St. Augustine," 25.

6. Langan, "Elements of St. Augustine," 24–25.

7. See Rhodes, *Making of the Atomic Bomb*, 592–600; and Batchelder, *Irreversible Decision*, 174–86.

8. Norman, *Ethics, Killing and War*, 1, 36–72.

government officials who were left in place by the Nazis were able to punish acts of anti-Semitism that the Nazis condoned. The Danish government protected the Jews there until Danish officials were forced to resign in 1943 when the Nazis took direct control of the country. But as the Nazis began a program to deport Jews to concentration camps, Danish officials alerted the Jewish community and were able to work secretly with the Danish resistance to save 95 percent of the Jewish population. Jews were hidden all over Denmark and then secretly ushered to Sweden, after Sweden made an *official pronouncement* that they would save Danish Jews from deportation. The vast majority of Danish Jews were saved.[9] As well, the aging king of Denmark, Christian X, often rode unaccompanied through Copenhagen as millions of his Danish subjects wore four coins tied together with red and white ribbons, a symbol of silent resistance to the Nazis.[10] In many cases, nonviolent resistance is not effective. But in Denmark, it accomplished amazing results.

Given Jesus' commands, the horror of modern warfare, and the possibility of effective and courageous nonviolent resistance, a strong case for pacifism can be made.

JUST WAR THEORY

While Augustine required a pacifist response in many cases, he also pointed out that in Romans 13 God appoints governing authorities and authorizes them to use force to promote peace and protect justice. Paul's discussion in Romans is worth quoting at length:

> Let everyone be subject to the governing authorities, for there is no authority except that which God has established . . . Consequently, whoever rebels against the authority is rebelling against what God has instituted, and those who do so will bring judgment on themselves. For rulers hold no terror for those who do right, but for those who do wrong. Do you want to be free from fear of the one in authority? Then do what is right and you will be commended. For the one in authority is God's servant to do you good. But if you do wrong, be afraid, for rulers do not bear the sword

---

9. United States Holocaust Memorial Museum, "Rescue in Denmark," paras. 3–4, sect. "Key Dates."

10. Mikkelson, "King of Denmark Wore"; and Editors of Encyclopedia Britannica, "Christian X: King."

for no reason. They are God's servants, agents of wrath to bring punishment on the wrongdoer. (Rom 13:1–4)

Here Paul is arguing that governing authorities were placed in their positions by God, and part of their calling is to reward good behavior and use force to punish evil, and by implication, create safety and peace for those in their jurisdiction by defending their subjects from evil. (For Paul to say governing authorities are established by God here is particularly arresting, since Roman rule was very oppressive of Israel at the time, and it was behind some of the persecutions Christians were experiencing.) Thus, in Rom 12 and 13, Paul seems to make a distinction between private violence in self-defense, which is not allowed, and officially sanctioned violence for (only) justified reasons.

Augustine uses Paul's statements to make the case, in *The City of God*, that part of a ruler's authority is to create a type of communal peace between people, *tranquillitas ordinis*, "the peace that springs from the just ordering of human affairs."[11] That is, a political peace that allows for the human flourishing of the governed.[12] It is part of the charity, or love for people, that the ruler ought to have. Here Augustine's arguments are compelling. Freedom from crime and freedom from unprovoked attack are part of the peace of the state. It seems hard to imagine that part of a ruler's calling would *not* be defending innocent civilians from crime or unwarranted attack, such as unprovoked invasion or terrorist violence. As Michael Uhlmann says, "Pacifism may be a desirable and, in certain circumstances, a compelling individual Christian response to violence or the threat of violence, but it cannot suffice as the governing moral criterion for a magistrate, who owes a duty in charity and justice to his subjects to protect them against the designs of evil men."[13] Defending the innocent against attack is part of the loving protection that a ruler must have for their subjects.

Therefore, in terms of justified cases of wartime self-defense, paradigmatic cases would include the Allied war against the Axis powers in World War II, and the U.S. defense of South Korea against the invasion from North Korea in 1950. In both the Axis and North Korean cases, the motivation for invasion appears to have been control of more territory. It seems, then, that part of a ruler's calling is to defend the innocent from

11. Uhlmann, "Use and Abuse of Just War Theory," para. 2.

12. Augustine discusses the temporal, political peace achievable by government rulers in his *City of God*, XV.4 and XIX.17.

13. Uhlmann, "Use and Abuse of Just War Theory," para. 2.

violence, including nation-states who invade, as well as terrorist acts like the suicide attacks on the World Trade Center on 9/11.

It also seems that, if a government is to employ pacifist resistance to an unprovoked invasion, the people of such a nation, on the whole, would need to agree to it. They would have to agree that the consequences of not using force to resist could mean hostile takeover, but that this is an acceptable price to pay for not employing violence.[14] It would seem unjust for a government to use only pacifistic resistance if the majority of the public is not behind it. This would mean that (many) people who do not hold pacifist principles would pay the price of invasion for the government's pacifistic convictions. Thus, in a democratic society, a presidential candidate must be clear before the election that he or she would use only nonviolent means against unwarranted invasions.

It seems then, that although war is a great evil, it is necessary in some (probably *very few*) clear cases of aggression in which the innocent will suffer. And while it is certainly the case that a government could misuse a self-defense ethic to justify a war (and many have), this does not impugn the doctrine itself. Simply because it can be misused, does not mean the right use of the doctrine isn't ethical. (A hammer can be misused for murder, but this does not mean that the sale of hammers is unethical.)

The right reasons for war, Augustine writes, have to do with *jus ad bellum* ("justice of war") and *jus in bello* ("justice *in* war").[15] That is, the war must be for just causes, and it must be executed in a just way.[16] Augustine's original ideas[17] have been modified today to include these principles: In *jus ad bellum* there are four criteria: (1) Only an official governing authority can carry out a war. Such a ruler must have recognized jurisdiction over a population and have as one of her aims the defense and proliferation of justice. In other words, an authority whose aim is peace within his or her state between its citizens, and peace between such a state and other states.[18]

---

14. Norman, *Ethics, Killing and War*, ch. 6.

15. For summaries of Augustine's just war theory, see Langan, "Elements of St. Augustine," 19–38; and Mattox, "Augustine: Political and Social Philosophy," paras. 2.a.–3.e.

16. Walzer's *Just and Unjust Wars* remains the standard on just war theory today. For summaries of just war theory used here, see Lazar, "War," Mattox, "Augustine: Political and Social Philosophy," sects. 2.a.–3.e.; Uhlmann, "Use and Abuse of Just War Theory"; and Moseley, "Just War Theory."

17. Not all of Augustine's criteria for just war are relevant today. See Langan, "Elements of St. Augustine," 21–23, 36.

18. Johnson, "Just War, As It Was," para. 2.

Private citizens are thus not a competent authority. (2) The war must be for a just cause. Augustine's original ideas have been modified by Thomas Aquinas (AD 1225–1274), and modern ethicists to emphasize that a war must be for defensive purposes, the righting of a wrong such as unprovoked attack by another country, the retaking of stolen property, etc. Defending an ally is also allowed. (3) The war must be fought with the right intentions. It must have peace as its ultimate aim, and not be fought for revenge, greed, or pursuit of glory and power. It must not be a provocative action in order to initiate hostilities. And finally, (4) The war must be fought with a probability of success. That is, it is unethical to engage in war if there is no hope of victory, or the aims of the war cannot be reasonably achieved. To these criteria recent ethicists have added: (5) War must be a last resort. All other means of achieving peace, such as diplomatic talks or economic sanctions, must be exhausted.[19] (This represents a significant modification of Augustine's view.)[20]

Jus in bello requires the war to be carried out in a just manner. (1) Civilians or non-combatants cannot be targeted, and civilian casualties must be accidental. Bombings must be of military targets only. (2) The military actions taken should be proportional. That is, the unintended harm to innocent lives and civilian infrastructure should be no more than is necessary to achieve the military objective. And (3) "The least harmful means feasible must be used." That is, weapons used should not be more destructive than necessary.[21] Modern ethicists have added: (4) Prisoners of war should be treated humanely. Torture or execution of surrendered combatants is not allowed.[22]

We can thus take elements of just war theory and combine them with elements of pacifism to defend a middle ground: that a strong presumption against violence must be the starting point, as human life is valuable, made in God's image, and once a life is taken it cannot be recovered.[23] Also, given modern technology's ease at destroying large numbers of people, both combatants and civilians, war must be a last resort. This is a different

---

19. Moseley, "Just War Theory," sect. "2. The Jus Ad Bellum Convention."
20. Johnson, "Just War, As It Was," para. 31.
21. Lazar, "War," 2.5.
22. United Nations, "Geneva Convention," sect. "Part II. General Protection of Prisoners of War."
23. Norman defends a "strong presumption against violence," but does not use Christian arguments. Norman, *Ethics, Killing and War*, 1–72. He ends the book in a stalemate between pacifist principles and limited just war reasoning, 207–53.

SECTION III: CHRISTIANITY IN *TREK*

beginning assumption than Augustine uses in his arguments. Augustine begins with the duty of a ruler to procure a measure of public peace and flourishing for the governed. But it seems to me that we must begin with a presumption against violence and make the criteria for a just war a high bar to achieve, given Jesus' commands to love our enemy, and the horrors of modern warfare.[24]

Recent ethicists such as Richard Norman have defended this view. Norman argues that since on the face of it, it is always wrong to harm, injure, or kill others, there must be strong reasons to overrule such a presumption of nonviolence.[25] In practice, this means we must make good-faith efforts to exhaust all possible peaceful solutions, including diplomacy, sanctions, and other less forceful means. On these criteria, most wars throughout history would qualify as unjust wars since they were either fought for the wrong reasons or carried out in an unjust manner.

In rough application of these principles, then, the Allied war against the Axis powers in World War II and the U.S. defense of South Korea in 1950 would exemplify just defenses against unprovoked invasion. The U.S. entry into the Korean War was just because we aided South Korea against an unprovoked invasion by North Korea. However, the Vietnam War and the war in Iraq after 9/11 are seen by many theorists as unjust wars. In the case of Vietnam we interfered in a civil war without invitation by either side.[26] And in the case of the Iraq War we did not have strong enough evidence that Iraq was building weapons of mass destruction. Thus there was no imminent threat to the United States.[27]

IS IT ETHICAL TO USE NUCLEAR WEAPONS?

The use of nuclear weapons poses a complex problem. The U.S. dropped two atomic weapons[28] on Japanese cities in 1945 and leveled them both. Somewhere between 129,000 and 226,000 people, mostly civilians, were killed.

---

24. Johnson, "Just War, As It Was," paras. 21, 24–26.
25. Norman, *Ethics, Killing and War*, 1–72.
26. For a discussion of the Vietnam war as unjust, see Walzer, *Just and Unjust Wars*, 97–101.
27. For arguments that the Iraq war was an unjust war, see Enemark and Michaelsen, "Just War Doctrine," 545–63; and DeCosse, "Totaling Up," paras. 1–9.
28. Nuclear weapons, which use nuclear fusion, are the weapons used today. But the atomic bombs dropped on Japan used nuclear *fission*, not fusion.

Was it right to drop the bombs on Japan? Michael Walzer argues that, given the unique nature of atomic weapons, the U.S. owed Japan "an experiment in negotiation," an extraordinary effort at peace before using the bomb. However, there was no evidence Japan would have listened or negotiated. The Japanese military leadership was very much against surrender, even after firebombing of their major cities, and even after the second atomic bomb was dropped on Nagasaki.[29] Casualties of an invasion of Japan proper would have been incredibly high on both sides. The invasion of Okinawa had cost 12,500 American lives (80,000 casualties) and 120,000 Japanese lives,[30] almost all of the latter killed in the fighting. Very few Japanese soldiers had surrendered. Potential American casualties in an invasion of Japan were estimated to be between 500,000 and 4 million.[31]

There were also doubts about how effective the atomic bomb would be because it hadn't been dropped in a wartime situation yet. What if the U.S. had warned Japan more strongly and negotiated, and then the bomb had not been effective, or been a dud? What if the U.S. staged a demonstration in Japan in a non-populated area, such as a desert, and it didn't show the real destructive capability of the bomb, hardening Japanese leaders into not surrendering?

Also, at the time it was unclear what devastation would result from dropping the bomb (although it was strongly suspected that it would be very destructive. Before dropping the bomb, Truman had written in his diary that we had discovered "the most terrible bomb in the history of the world," and compared it to the Bible's apocalyptic description of the world's end by fire).[32] Nevertheless, Truman was still not sure how much devastation would result from the bomb, and at the time he did not know the torturous deaths that Japanese people would die who were not immediately killed by the blast. People died horrible, slow deaths due to massive burns and exposure to radiation, but at the time it wasn't clear how the bomb would affect a population. (But given what we *now know* about how people die due to atomic or nuclear weapons, it seems that it is *now* unjust to use nuclear weapons, because of their torturous effects. People who are not at ground zero, who die in the coming days and weeks, die horrible deaths.) Given what Truman knew and did not know at the time, the dropping of

---

29. See Rhodes, *Making of the Atomic Bomb*, 687–88, 743–44.
30. Walzer, *Just and Unjust Wars*. 266; and Rhodes, *Making of the Atomic Bomb*, 687.
31. Cox, "H-057–1," sect. "Operation Downfall."
32. Rhodes, *Making of the Atomic Bomb*, 690.

the bomb was a measure effected to save both American and Japanese lives to end the war quickly.

However, U.S. use of the bomb on Japanese cities was only justified by American commanders because the Allies were already firebombing cities and targeting civilians. Firebombing, or "carpet-bombing," as it was called, began as an Allied strategy in 1943 with the bombing of Hamburg, Germany. Incendiary bombs set the whole city on fire and destroyed it, killing at least 45,000 Germans, mostly children and the elderly.[33] A top-secret British order, No. 173, explicitly ordered the destruction of *all* of Hamburg, not just military targets. It was the first time that civilian casualties were an explicit Allied strategy to win the war.[34] In the months before dropping the bomb on Hiroshima, 100,000 people had died in the firebombing of Tokyo, and this was comparable to the estimated 110,000 to 210,000 people who died in both Hiroshima and Nagasaki when atomic bombs were used on these cities later.[35]

By the time Truman decided to drop the bomb on Japan, a psychological barrier had already been crossed. We were already killing thousands of civilians through firebombing as a strategy to hurt the "morale" of the enemy and end the war.[36] By August of 1945, the U.S. had already firebombed fifty-eight Japanese cities.[37] Because of this, only a half-hearted effort was made to find primarily military targets for the atomic bomb. Some targets were primarily military and others were not. Hiroshima was bombed on August 6, and Nagasaki on August 9, 1945. Although on August 9, the number one target for the bomb was Kokura Arsenal, a military target, it was hidden by cloud cover (so U.S. pilots couldn't acquire the target), and American bombers started to meet Japanese resistance. Because of this the pilots flew to Nagasaki, their second target, and dropped the bomb there. The pilots didn't want to ditch the bomb in the ocean or try to bring it back.[38] Nagasaki, "the San Francisco of Japan," was utterly destroyed by the bomb. Richard Rhodes believes a major reason Nagasaki made it on the

---

33. Rhodes, *Making of the Atomic Bomb*, 474.

34. Rhodes, *Making of the Atomic Bomb*, 471–72.

35. Walzer, *Just and Unjust Wars*, 266; and Wellerstein, "Counting the Dead," sect. "So What Numbers?"

36. Rhodes, *Making of the Atomic Bomb*, 471, 475.

37. Rhodes, *Making of the Atomic Bomb*, 687.

38. Rhodes, *Making of the Atomic Bomb*, 739–40.

target list was simply because it was one of the few large cities that had not been firebombed by the Allies.[39]

Truman denied in his diary that he targeted civilians when dropping the bomb, and he did ask which Japanese cities were used exclusively for wartime production.[40] But as Walzer points out, this was "reflexive . . . It is possible to ask such questions only when the answer doesn't matter," he says.[41] Truman was not serious about such considerations because he would have bombed cities whether they had military installations or not, and it was ridiculous to think that there were cities that were *exclusively* military targets.[42] We do know Truman felt guilty about dropping the devices afterward because of the debate about dropping a third bomb on Japan when Japan didn't immediately surrender after the second bomb was dropped. According to Henry Wallace, Truman's secretary of commerce, who was in on the discussions:

> Truman said he had given orders to stop the atomic bombing. He said the thought of wiping out another 100,000 people was too horrible. He didn't like the idea of killing, he said, "all those kids."[43]

According to principles of *jus in bello*, the firebombing *and* the dropping of the atomic weapons by the Allies were unjust. Under principle one, it is never right to target civilians or use civilian casualties as part of a wartime strategy. Certainly, the effort to end the war quickly and save the lives of American soldiers was commendable and understandable. But the ends don't justify the means. Civilian deaths should never be a wartime strategy. Only primarily military targets should have been used.

Given what Truman knew at the time, it wasn't unjust to use the bomb at all, it was unjust to use it as a strategy to kill civilians. Today, knowing what we know about how people die torturous deaths from the use of nuclear weapons, it seems unjust to drop nuclear weapons at all.

What of the soldier's responsibility in war? Should a soldier resist going to war if the war is unjust? Augustine argues that a soldier's position "makes obedience a duty." That is, even if the ruler is unjust or gives an

39. Rhodes, *Making of the Atomic Bomb*, 689.
40. Rhodes, *Making of the Atomic Bomb*, 690–91.
41. Walzer, *Just and Unjust Wars*, 265.
42. Walzer, *Just and Unjust Wars*, 265–66.
43. Walzer, *Just and Unjust Wars*, 743.

SECTION III: CHRISTIANITY IN *TREK*

"unrighteous command," it is the soldier's responsibility to obey his or her superiors and leave the justification of the war up to them. This makes the soldier's participation innocent, regardless of the reasons for the war.[44] Augustine mentions Luke 3:14 here, in which a soldier asks John the Baptist what he should do.[45] John doesn't tell him to resign his commission. Instead, he tells him to use his position justly, not accusing people falsely or extorting money. Thus, the soldier can carry out his duties in a just way.

Returning to "Bread and Circuses," we can now see a strong Christian presumption against using violence, and Flavius' convictions about not fighting in the arena are justified. Jesus did say to turn the other cheek. But we can also see how Flavius instinctively resorted to a defensive posture when he was put back into the games. When he did his best to protect Spock and McCoy in the arena, this is analogous in some ways to a ruler's defense of an innocent population for which he or she is responsible.

KIRK AND SLAVERY

KIRK: Our people don't believe in slavery.

In the scene in which Kirk and his landing party are brought before Septimus, the head of the runaway slaves and a "brother of the Son," Kirk declares that in the Federation slavery is wrong. The enslaving of sentient creatures anywhere in the galaxy is a gross evil.

This makes Kirk's decision to sleep with the slave woman Claudius provided all the more appalling. What hypocrisy! While Kirk said he doesn't believe in slavery, he apparently thinks it is okay to sleep with a slave who is provided to him for his "pleasure," and who has no choice but to please him. It goes without saying that if slavery is wrong, it applies to a beautiful, alluring slave as much as it applies to any other slave.

Claudius tells Kirk the next day, "Because you are a man, I gave you some last hours as a man." This fits with the masculine stereotypes that are abundantly provided in *The Original Series*. It's not just that a man ought to be strong and courageous, defending his ship and crew. A true "man" ought to take advantage of any beautiful woman he can, on any planet he visits. Kirk does this in spades. His womanizing in *The Original Series* is a stark example of what men ought *not* to do.

---

44. Langan, "Elements of St. Augustine," 23.
45. Langan, "Elements of St. Augustine," 24.

SECTION IV

Messianic Themes in *Trek*

INTRODUCTION

SOME OF THE MOST interesting and beautifully written *Star Trek* stories are echoes of messianic themes in the Bible. "The Messiah" was the promised one in the Old Testament who would be descended from David and save Israel from its sins. In the New Testament, Jesus of Nazareth is identified as the Messiah, and he was crucified as a substitute for the sins of the world. He sacrificed himself to save others.

In this section we explore "The Empath" (TOS), in which an alien woman named Gem offers to sacrifice her life to save Kirk, Spock, and McCoy. In so doing, she saves her entire planet in true messianic fashion. Here we'll take a closer look at the concept of the messiah and the predictions of a sacrificial messiah in Isaiah chapter 53.

In the *Star Trek II* and *III* films, Spock sacrifices his life to save the *Enterprise* crew, and then he is resurrected on the Genesis Planet, much like Jesus sacrificed himself for others and was raised again on the third day. Here we'll take a closer look at whether it is rational to believe in the resurrection of Jesus.

There is more messianic content in volume 2, where we will explore Captain Sisko as a messianic figure in *Deep Space Nine*, and Hemmer as a messianic figure in "All Those Who Wander" (SNW).

Many *Star Trek* stories have messianic themes and symbols, and they are some of the most powerful and memorable stories in the *Trek* canon.

9

Priceless Gem

"The Empath" (*The Original Series*)

WATCH "THE EMPATH" (TOS SEASON 3)

THE *ENTERPRISE* IS CHECKING on a Starfleet observation post on a planet whose sun will go supernova within hours and destroy the entire solar system. Kirk, Spock, and McCoy beam down to investigate. The station is deserted, and when they replay the last security tapes from the facility, they witness a small earthquake that occurs, prompting one scientist on the tape to quote Ps 95:4: "In his hand are the deep places of the earth." There is a high-pitched noise, and abruptly both scientists disappear in a flurry of colored light. Kirk, Spock, and McCoy then experience a similar noise, and they disappear in the same way. Spock discovers that they were transported roughly a hundred meters beneath the surface by an advanced transporter.

When they arrive, they see a woman reclining on a couch in the shape of a cross. She cannot speak, and Dr. McCoy discovers that she has no vocal cords. She is a mute, and they decide to call her "Gem." Gem reaches out to touch a cut on Kirk's forehead. The cut disappears, reappears on Gem's forehead, then disappears from hers. She is an "empath," someone who can take on both the emotions and the physical wounds of another onto herself. Kirk is healed.

Suddenly, two strange, cerebral-looking aliens appear, telling them that they are "Vians" and to not interfere. They trap Kirk, Spock, and McCoy behind a forcefield to check on Gem, then turn off the forcefield and leave. Through a series of events, it becomes clear that the Vians, through their "experiments," tortured and killed the two Federation scientists who disappeared earlier, and they now want to experiment on Kirk and his crew. Kirk offers himself to the Vians so Spock, McCoy, and Gem would be spared. He is tortured as his arms are handcuffed to chains which are stretched out and hung from the ceiling. The Vians want no information. When they are finished with Kirk, Gem and the others appear, and Gem touches his wounds, healing Kirk. Later, the Vians tell him they must do more experiments, which could be deadly, on one of his two men. Kirk must decide which one, Spock or McCoy, will be the test subject. McCoy tricks Kirk and Spock, injecting them with sedatives, and both men are knocked out. He then offers himself to the Vians, and he is horribly tortured. When Kirk and the others rejoin him afterward, McCoy has massive internal injuries and will not survive.

The Vians appear and watch Gem closely. They explain that there are several planets destined for destruction in the solar system, and they can save the population of only one. They are doing the experiment to see if Gem will sacrifice her life to save the others, thus proving her people worthy of being rescued. They tell Kirk and Spock, "Each of you is willing to give his life for the others. We must now find out whether that instinct has been transmitted to Gem." While Gem touches McCoy and takes on some of his wounds, she is afraid to take on the more dangerous ones. But Kirk and Spock argue with the Vians that she really *has* offered her life to save them. They finally acquiesce. They mercifully heal McCoy, then disappear with Gem.

Back on the *Enterprise* bridge, Kirk, McCoy, and Spock are telling Scotty about their unusual adventure. Scotty describes Jesus' parable of the "Pearl of Great Price." A man finds a pearl of limitless value and sells all he has to buy the land with the pearl in it. They all agree that Gem is that pearl of great price.

WORLDVIEW ANALYSIS

"The Empath" is full of rich Christian imagery and messianic themes. Joyce Muskat wrote the Christian themes in the story, bookending the episode with quotes from the Bible.[1]

---

1. Joyce Muskat, in discussion with the author, June 30, 2023.

Priceless Gem

OZABA [SCIENTIST]: In his hand are the deep places of the earth. Psalm ninety-five, verse four. Looks like he was listening.

This dialogue occurs in the teaser to the story, when Kirk, Spock, and McCoy are replaying the security tapes of the planet's observation post. An earthquake shakes the ground as their sun's run-up to a supernova continues to affect the planet. One of the scientists quotes Ps 95, saying it "looks like he was listening," clearly a reference to God. The reference here to "the deep places of the earth" also has a double meaning. It refers to the earthquakes, but it also foreshadows that the Vians will trap Kirk and his friends deep in their underground facility.

[They find Gem reclining on a couch in the shape of a cross.]

This episode has fascinating crucifixion imagery. First, Kirk, Spock, and McCoy find Gem lying on a couch in the shape of a cross. The cross foreshadows Gem's sacrifice for the trio and the salvation of her planet. Also, when Kirk and McCoy are tortured, their hands are hanging from chains in the ceiling, spreading out their arms as if hanging on a cross.[2] Muskat says she did not include this imagery in her script, and it was undoubtedly added during the production.[3] Thus the combination of her script and the production of the episode beautifully pictures Jesus' death (see below).

GEM AND ISAIAH 53

McCOY: She's a mute, Jim. No vocal cords, not even vestigals.

Larry Kreitzer points out that just as Gem is a mute and cannot defend herself, so Jesus did not speak in his own defense at his trial. Kreitzer refers to the predictions of Jesus' silence in Isaiah chapter 53.[4] Isaiah is a book of the Bible that we know was written several hundred years before Jesus' birth because the Great Isaiah Scroll, part of the Dead Sea Scrolls, was discovered in 1946. This scroll was chemically dated to between 351–53 BC.[5] Isa 53:7 says:

---

2. Kreitzer, "Suffering, Sacrifice," 144.
3. Muskat, discussion.
4. Kreitzer, "Suffering, Sacrifice," 145–47.
5. See VanderKam and Flint, *Meaning of the Dead Sea Scrolls*, 31. For scholarly defenses of Isaiah's authorship of both parts of the book of Isaiah, see Harrison, *Introduction to the Old Testament*, 764–800; and Oswalt, *Book of Isaiah*, 17–28.

Section IV: Messianic Themes in *Trek*

He was oppressed and afflicted, yet he did not open his mouth;
He was led like a lamb to the slaughter, and as a sheep before its shearers is silent, so he did not open his mouth.[6]

This parallels the description of Jesus' silence at his trial in Mark 14:60:

Then the high priest stood up before them and asked Jesus, "Are you not going to answer? What is this testimony that these men are bringing against you?" But Jesus remained silent and gave no answer.

Jesus did not defend himself because it was his plan, and the plan of God the Father, to sacrifice his life for the forgiveness of the world. Rev 13:8 says, for example, that Jesus was slain "from the creation of the world." Therefore, Jesus willingly went to his death because it was God's eternal plan to sacrifice him for the world's sins.

McCOY: The wound is completely healed. It fits, Jim. She must be an empath . . . She can actually feel our emotional and physical reactions. They become part of her.

In this scene, Kirk has a cut on his forehead and Gem touches his wound. The wound then appears on her forehead before it disappears and is healed. She literally took on Kirk's wound and healed it.

This parallels Isa 53:5,[7] which says:

But he was wounded for our transgressions,
    crushed for our iniquities;
upon him was the punishment that made us whole,
    and by his bruises we are healed. (NRSV)

Here the Messiah takes on the wounds of others and heals them, just like Gem. He took the sins and wounds of the world onto himself (see below).

[KIRK is stripped to the waist, his arms stretched out and hanging from chains. As he is tortured, Gem watches.]

The torture scenes in "The Empath" are hard to watch. In 1968 when the episode first aired, there were objections to showing these scenes on network television. NBC decided not to repeat the episode in the summer of 1969 because it was too violent for the 7:30 p.m. time slot. And in

---

6. For the debate about whether Isa 53 refers to Jesus, see below.
7. Kreitzer, "Suffering, Sacrifice," 147.

England, the episode was banned because of the torture scenes and was not aired there until 1994.[8]

> SPOCK: It is complete. Gem has earned the right of survival for her planet. She offered her life.

Here Spock recognizes that Gem has offered her life to save McCoy, something that the Vians come to realize as well. She is willing to lay down her life for all three of the men.

Kreitzer points out that John 15 has an apt description of Gem's role here. In it, Jesus says, "Love each other as I have loved you. Greater love has no one than this: to lay one's life down for one's friends" (John 15:12–13).[9] At the end of the episode, Gem has learned self-sacrifice from the three men. She witnessed each of them offering to sacrifice himself for the sake of the other two: First, early on, Kirk tells the Vians to take him in his friends' stead, and they torture him. Later, Spock decides to sacrifice himself for the other two after McCoy knocks Kirk out with a sedative. But then McCoy is able to get the best of both Spock and Kirk when he puts Spock to sleep the same way he did Kirk. McCoy then decides to sacrifice himself. In the end, although Gem struggles with taking on all of McCoy's internal injuries, Spock is right: She has passed the Vians' test and is willing to give up her life. Her sacrifice and love for the others literally save her entire people. Thus, each of the four characters in the story demonstrates Jesus' love, a self-sacrificial love.

THE MESSIAH AND SELF-SACRIFICE

Gem's willingness to give her life for the others is a reflection of Jesus' sacrificial death to save the world from sin. Jesus' sacrifice is "messianic" in the sense that Jesus was the Promised One who would come and save Israel from its sins (Matt 1:20–21, Luke 1:26–38). The word "messiah" means "anointed one."[10]

Incredibly, Jesus' sacrifice was again predicted in Isa 53, which speaks of the "suffering servant," the Messiah. Although there have been attempts to explain the "suffering servant" here as not referring to an individual, it's very likely that it does refer to an individual here. For one thing, many

---

8. Cushman, *Voyages: TOS Season Three*, 251.
9. See Kreitzer, "Suffering, Sacrifice," 141.
10. See Evans, "Messianism," 698–707.

ancient rabbinic sources believed Isa 53 was referring to an individual.[11] For another, when New Testament writers declared that Isa 53 was referring to Jesus, they used Jewish methods of interpreting Old Testament prophecies that were common at the time, known as *midrashic* and *pesher* exegesis.[12]

When we take a look at Isa 53, the similarities between what it describes and Jesus' sacrifice for sin are truly remarkable:

> [5] But he was wounded for our transgressions,
>   crushed for our iniquities;
> upon him was the punishment that made us whole,
>   and by his bruises we are healed.
> [6] . . . the Lord has laid on him
>   the iniquity of us all . . .
> [8] By a perversion of justice he was taken away.
>   Who could have imagined his future?
> For he was cut off from the land of the living,
>   stricken for the transgression of my people.
> [9] They made his grave with the wicked and his tomb with the rich,
>   although he had done no violence, and there was no deceit in his mouth.
> [10] Yet it was the will of the Lord to crush him with pain.
> When you make his life an offering for sin,
>   he shall see his offspring, and shall prolong his days;
> through him the will of the Lord shall prosper.
> [11] . . . The righteous one, my servant, shall make many righteous,
>   and he shall bear their iniquities. (Isa 53:5–11 NRSV)

There is a lot to unpack from these verses. First, we see a substitutionary death by the Messiah to pay for the sins of the world. Phrases such as "he was wounded for our transgressions," "upon him was the punishment that made us whole," "the Lord laid on him the iniquity of us all," and the Lord "crushed him with pain" all refer to a substitutionary offering that the Messiah performed in humanity's place, known as an *atonement*.[13] The word "atonement" in the Old Testament refers to an animal sacrifice that pays for the sins of the people. Here the phrase "make his life an offering for sin" is a translation of the Hebrew word *asam*, which means "guilt offering," the same word that is used in Lev 5–7, in the instructions for the sacrifice

---

11. Brown, "Jewish Interpretations," 62–64.
12. See Longnecker, *Biblical Exegesis*, 6–35.
13. For a discussion of the language here referring to substitutionary atonement, see Allen, "Substitutionary Atonement," 171–89.

that the Israelites were to give to God to cover their sins. Since there are two other Hebrew words in this passage that are also in Lev 5–7, it is clear here that the Messiah would be a "guilt offering" for the people.[14]

Then we see that the Messiah was "taken away" by a "perversion of justice." He was "cut off from the land of the living" and was given a "grave with the wicked" even though he had "done no violence" and "no deceit was in his mouth." He was innocent, but he was considered wicked and crucified, as the Gospels report (Mark 14:62–65, 15:9–15). Then he was given a "tomb with the rich" when he died (Mark 15:42–46).

In verse 11 of Isa 53, it says the Messiah shall "make many righteous and he shall bear their iniquities." Alec Motyer explains here that the Hebrew phrase "make righteous" is unique in the Old Testament and can be translated "bring righteousness to" or "provide righteousness for." He goes on to say:

> In a context where the Servant's *personal righteousness* receives such emphasis, the phrase, "to provide righteousness for the many" can mean only that there are those ("the many") *whom he clothes in righteousness*, sharing with them his own perfect acceptability before God.[15]

Amazingly, because of the Messiah's sacrifice for sin, God now offers everyone the gift of the Messiah's righteousness. It is available for anyone who receives it, and it makes them acceptable in God's sight.

Interestingly, verse 10 says "he shall see his offspring and shall prolong his days." The precise meaning of this line is debated by scholars, but one possible interpretation, defended by Motyer and Allen, is that it refers to the Messiah returning to life.[16]

ATONEMENT FOR SIN

The apostle Paul picks up these themes from Isaiah in his letter to the Romans. In a fascinating passage, Rom 3:24–25 says that "God presented [Jesus] as a sacrifice of atonement," which allowed us to be "justified freely by

---

14. Allen, "Substitutionary Atonement," 179.

15. Motyer, *Prophecy of Isaiah*, 442, emphasis mine.

16. There are several possible interpretations here, but Motyer and Allen defend a resurrection interpretation. See Motyer, *Prophecy of Isaiah*, 440–41; and Allen, "Substitutionary Atonement," 179.

his grace through the redemption that came by Christ Jesus." Several words in this passage are key for understanding Christian belief.

The Greek word for "atonement" here, *hilasterion*, refers to the "mercy seat" on top of the ark of the covenant, upon which the blood of the sacrifice was sprinkled during a special holiday in Israel called the Day of Atonement. Thus, *hilasterion* refers to a "guilt offering," an "atonement," which covered the sins of the people of Israel for that year and also turned aside God's wrath regarding sin.[17] (Recall that in chapter 5 we saw that God's wrath is very different than the wrath of pagan gods.) Therefore, Jesus' atonement pays for our sins and satisfies God's justice.[18]

Paul's term "justified" is a legal term, which means to be "declared righteous." It's as if humanity is prosecuted in a court of law for its sins, and for everyone who believes in Jesus' sacrifice, they are declared "not guilty."[19] The connection to Isaiah's phrase, "make the many righteous," is clear.

Paul's phrase "freely by his grace" is a theme he undoubtedly picks up from Isa 55:1–2. His phrase means that God justifies people as a *free gift*, not because of anything they have earned.[20] Since it's impossible to be sin-free,[21] no one can earn their way to become righteous and be worthy of God's acceptance. It is by God's own plan, which he originated in eternity because he loved humanity, that he declares people "not guilty" (Eph 1:4–6, Rom 3:24). In other words, God does all the work to save us. We simply accept his gift by "faith." In Rom 4 it says, "Now to the one who works, wages are not credited as a gift but as an obligation. However, to the one who does not work but trusts God who justifies the ungodly, their faith is credited as righteousness" (Rom 4:4–5). In other words, by accepting Jesus' death as a sacrifice for their sins, anyone can be declared "righteous" by God.[22] Because such persons are clean before him, they can enter a relation-

---

17. See Moo's discussion in his *Letter to the Romans*, 231–37, in which he discusses *hilasterion* and the differences between God's wrath and pagan conceptions of wrath. For background on the Day of Atonement, see Hartley, "Atonement, Day of," 54–61.

18. For biblical explanations of atonement see Rom 3:25–26 and Heb 9:1—10:18. For an academic defense of the idea that Jesus' death "paid for our sins," see Porter, "Swinburnian Atonement," 228–41.

19. Moo, *Letter to the Romans*, 227.

20. Moo, *Letter to the Romans*, 228–29.

21. See Paul's argument in Rom 2:1—3:20.

22. Accepting Jesus' forgiveness for our sins implies that we want to stop sinning, and "repentance" is the theological term for desiring to stop sinning.

ship with him that lasts to eternity (John 3:16–17, 17:3). Amazingly, it is all *God's* doing.

Paul's word "redemption" means "liberation by the payment of a price." It is as if humanity has been "kidnapped" by sin, or "enslaved" to sin, and Jesus paid the price to free the world.[23] That is why this message is called the "gospel," which means, "good news."

Finally, Gem's sacrifice in "The Empath" also reflects a theme Joyce Muskat discovered known as "The Answerer," which was the original title of her script.[24] "[The Answerer is] an Egyptian concept where a person goes to a judge and says, 'I answer for him,' and the person he is answering for gets punishment or reward based on the answers that were given," she said. "Gem, in a way, answers for Spock and McCoy when they are injured. She wants to save them."[25] The overlap between the meaning of Jesus' sacrifice and the "Answerer" is clear. For Muskat the episode reflects both themes.[26]

> SCOTTY: She was a pearl of great price . . . Do you not know the story of the merchant? The merchant, who when he found one pearl of great price, went and sold all that he had and bought it?

The episode ends with another reference to Scripture. Here Scotty describes Jesus' parable known as the "Pearl of Great Price." In Matt 13:45–46 it says:

> Again, the kingdom of heaven is like a merchant looking for fine pearls. When he found one of great value [the "Pearl of Great Price"], he went away and sold everything he had and bought it.

In the parable, the kingdom of God ("kingdom of heaven" is another phrase meaning the same thing) is so valuable, a person who discovers it is willing to give up everything they have to get it. The implication is that the person receives the kingdom "with great joy," as in Matt 13:44.[27] The sacrifice made for experiencing the kingdom is small indeed compared to the joy it brings. Here it is important to note that this passage is not talking about earning entrance into the kingdom, because salvation is a free gift from God (see above). Rather, it refers to a person's willingness to give up

---

23. See Moo's discussion in *Letter to the Romans*, 229–30.
24. Muskat, discussion, and Cushman, *Voyages: TOS Season Three*, 233.
25. Cushman, *Voyages: TOS Season Three*, 233.
26. Muskat, discussion.
27. Hagner, *Matthew 1–13*, 396–97.

their way of life (endure persecution or lose their job, for example), in order to experience the beauty of the kingdom.

In this final scene, Scotty declares Gem is a "pearl of great price" and Kirk agrees. "Yes, she was all that," Kirk says. "And whether the Vians bought her or found her makes little difference. She was of great value."

10

Resurrection and Rebirth
Star Trek II and *Star Trek III* Films
(*The Original Series*)

WATCH THE *STAR TREK II* AND *STAR TREK III* FILMS

The *Star Trek II* and *III* movies, which feature the TOS cast, combine to form one story of the sacrifice, death, and resurrection of Spock, making him a strong messianic character in the films. In *Star Trek II*, we learn of the Genesis Project, a top secret Federation experiment to create "life from lifelessness." The technology takes a barren, lifeless planet and transforms the molecular structure there into living forms, both plants and animals. The potential to create habitable planets from uninhabitable worlds is stunning. But if the Genesis Device is used on living life forms, it destroys such life as it creates new molecular structures. Thus it could be used to destroy *all* life on entire planets. Kirk's former flame, scientist Carol Marcus, heads the project.

Chekov, who is now part of the crew of the USS *Reliant*, is part of the Genesis Project's search for a lifeless world on which to test the Genesis Device. Instead of finding a lifeless planet, Chekov and Captain Terrell of the *Reliant* inadvertently beam down to Ceti Alpha V, a world in which Kirk had allowed his nemesis Khan Noonien Singh and his followers to settle years before in the TOS episode "Space Seed." Khan blames Kirk for his wife's death and the deaths of other settlers when a series of disasters afflicted the planet months after Kirk left them there. Khan forcibly finds out the top secret information about Genesis from Chekov and Terrell. He then decides to hijack the *Reliant*, get Genesis, and take his revenge on Kirk. During the ensuing duel between Kirk and Khan, Kirk meets his grown son David Marcus, a son he had with Carol Marcus years before.

Through a series of battles between the *Enterprise* and Khan's *Reliant*, Kirk gets the best of Khan and demands he surrender. But Khan will not be beaten. He begins detonation of the Genesis Device, which he has on board his ship. The crippled *Enterprise* cannot move away fast enough to get outside the upcoming blast radius. Spock, knowing the warp drive is offline, hurries down to engineering to repair it. But he must enter a sealed compartment full of radiation, and McCoy won't let him in, saying, "Are you out of your Vulcan mind? No human can tolerate the radiation that's in there!" Spock replies, "But, as you are so fond of observing, Doctor, I'm not human." He knocks out McCoy with a Vulcan nerve pinch and does a quick mind meld with him. He then enters the compartment and fixes the warp drive but is exposed to lethal doses of radiation. The *Enterprise*, able to get out of danger, warps to safety as the Genesis Device explodes. But Spock is mortally wounded. "Do not grieve, Admiral," he tells Kirk. "The needs of the many outweigh the needs of the few." Spock dies before Kirk's eyes. Spock's casket, a photon torpedo tube, is jettisoned at his funeral as *Amazing Grace* is played in the background. It lands on the newly formed Genesis Planet, offering some hope that Spock could return.

In *Star Trek III*, we learn that in Spock's last-minute mind meld with McCoy, he gave McCoy his *katra*, his immaterial soul, as Vulcan tradition requires when a Vulcan is near death. McCoy starts displaying signs of mental illness as he houses his own soul and Spock's at the same time. Sarek, Spock's father, tells Kirk that he must get Spock's body and his *katra* back to Vulcan. It is the only way to save Spock's soul in the Vulcan way. Kirk realizes that he must return to the Genesis Planet to recover whatever is left of Spock's body there and bring it, along with McCoy, back to Vulcan. Kirk then steals the decommissioned *Enterprise* to get back to the Genesis Planet. In the meantime, Lt. Saavik and David Marcus arrive at the planet, and they find a young Vulcan boy near Spock's casket. Spock's body has regenerated, and he is now a growing young Vulcan. But in a melee with Klingons, who arrive at the Genesis Planet to attempt to steal the Genesis Device for themselves, Kirk's son David is killed. Kirk is able to retrieve

Resurrection and Rebirth

Spock and Saavik unharmed, however. Racing back to Vulcan, he arrives in time for an ancient and untested ceremony: to reunite Spock's *katra* with his (now fully grown) body. In the ceremony, McCoy identifies himself as the "son of David." The procedure is successful, and in the last scene, Spock finally recognizes Kirk as his friend. Spock has sacrificed his life to save the *Enterprise*, died, and was resurrected.

WORLDVIEW ANALYSIS

There are a host of biblical references in *Star Trek II* and *III*. Clearly the scriptwriters used creation and resurrection themes from Scripture to enrich their story.

> MCCOY: According to myth, the Earth was created in six days. Now, watch out! Here comes Genesis. We'll do it for you in six minutes!

There are several interesting aspects of this quotation. First, we see McCoy's ambivalence about the Genesis Project. It's not just that it has huge potential to transform uninhabitable planets into habitable ones. It can also be used as a superweapon to destroy all life on any already inhabited planet. This is the reason the Klingons tried to acquire it in *Star Trek III*, as well as Khan's motivation to blow up the Enterprise at the end of *Star Trek II*. The debate in the Federation on using the Genesis Device (if it had been successfully designed) would have followed the similar debate we saw about dropping the atomic bomb on Japan in World War II.[1]

Second, regarding the many biblical references in the story, Genesis, an obvious reference, is the first book of the Bible. It describes God's creation of the world (Gen 1–3). But there are other, more subtle references. In *Star Trek III*, Kirk calls the plan to get Spock and McCoy back to Vulcan the "promised land," a reference to the land in the Middle East that God promised to Abraham and the Israelites as a new place for them to settle.[2] As well, at Spock's funeral *Amazing Grace* is played on the bagpipes, a famous Christian hymn written by John Newton in the eighteenth century. And at the ceremony on Vulcan to unite Spock's *katra* with his body, McCoy

---

1. See ch. 8.

2. Genesis 12:1 is the first of many biblical references to the "promised land." See McKeown, "Land, Fertility, Famine," 488–91.

SECTION IV: MESSIANIC THEMES IN *TREK*

identifies himself as "Leonard McCoy, son of David." "Son of David" was a messianic title applied to Jesus in the New Testament.

> SPOCK: Don't grieve, Admiral . . . The needs of the many outweigh . . .
>
> KIRK: the needs of the few.
>
> SPOCK: Or the one.

In this story we have a beautiful reflection of the death and resurrection of Jesus. Spock sacrifices his life to save the *Enterprise* crew, and as *Amazing Grace* is played at his funeral and his casket is shot toward the Genesis Planet, we suspect he will return. He does. He is dead, buried, and resurrected.

As Kreitzer points out, Spock's sacrifice is a reflection of Jesus' own purpose to "give his life as a ransom for many."[3] We saw in the last chapter that Jesus was a sacrifice to pay for the sins of the world, and that this was predicted in Isa 53.[4]

PARALLELS BETWEEN SPOCK AND JESUS

> McCOY: Are you out of your Vulcan mind? No human can tolerate the radiation that's in there!
>
> SPOCK: But, as you are so fond of observing, Doctor, I'm not human.

In another parallel between Spock's and Jesus' deaths, Spock reminds McCoy that he is not human. It is possible that he can endure the radiation in the compartment and save the crew because he is part Vulcan, in the same way that Jesus is able to save us through his death because he has a different nature than us. According to Christian theology, Jesus is both fully God and fully human, and it is this special nature that allows him to pay the penalty for the sins of the world. The combination of his human and divine nature is known as the doctrine of the incarnation.[5]

Kreitzer also points out that when Spock does his brief mind meld with McCoy, giving McCoy his *katra*, he says, "Remember." This is reminiscent

---

3. Kreitzer, "Suffering, Sacrifice," 151; and Mark 10:45.
4. For the debate about whether Isa 53 refers to Jesus, see ch. 9.
5. On the incarnation, see Packer, "Incarnation," 501–4. For a defense of the logical coherence of the incarnation, see Morris, *Logic of God Incarnate*.

of Jesus' words to "do this in remembrance of me" when he partakes of the Last Supper with his disciples the night before he is killed. They eat the bread and drink the wine so they can remember Jesus' sacrifice.[6]

Of course, there are differences between Spock's sacrifice and Jesus' sacrifice. Jesus knew from early on that he would sacrifice himself for the world, while Spock made a last-minute decision to make his sacrifice. Spock's sacrifice doesn't pay for sins, of course. But the parallels between them are close enough to make Spock a messianic symbol.

JESUS' BURIAL CLOTHES

DAVID: Saavik... What is it?

SAAVIK: Spock's burial robe.

When David and Saavik find Spock's casket on the Genesis Planet, his body is not in it. Instead, his burial robe is left and his body has disappeared. This parallels the gospel accounts of Jesus' empty tomb. Jesus' body was not in the tomb, but his burial clothes were left behind. In John 20:6–8 it says:

> Then Simon Peter . . . went straight into the tomb. He saw the strips of linen lying there, as well as the cloth that had been around Jesus' head. The cloth was still lying in its place, separate from the linen. Finally, the other disciple [John], who had reached the tomb first, also went inside. He saw and believed.[7]

There has been some debate about what the disciples actually saw here. What we know is that Jesus' body was wrapped in strips of linen, and spices would have been applied to the strips and (very likely) hardened around the body. If someone had simply stolen the body, they undoubtedly would have taken the body, strips and all, given the difficulty of getting them off the body. And the spices would have been valuable to take. Instead, John reports that the strips that had been around Jesus' body were lying there, but it does not say *how* the linens were lying there. It merely says that the cloth around Jesus' head was folded neatly. Whatever all this looked like, apparently it was an unusual sight and led John to believe Jesus was resurrected.[8]

---

6. Kreitzer, "Suffering, Sacrifice," 155. See also Luke 22:19 and 1 Cor 11:24.
7. For the context to this passage, see John 20:3–9.
8. See Carson, *Gospel According to John*, 637–69.

SECTION IV: MESSIANIC THEMES IN *TREK*

THE HISTORICITY OF THE RESURRECTION

SAAVIK: It is Doctor Marcus' opinion that this is . . . that the Genesis effect has in some way regenerated . . . Captain Spock.

Spock comes back to life as his body is regenerated on the Genesis Planet. We first see him as a boy eight to twelve years of age. Again, this echoes the accounts of Jesus' resurrection in the Gospels, although, in those accounts, Jesus comes back as an adult.

Here it is important to note the importance of the resurrection in Christian theology, as well as the lines of evidence that support Jesus' bodily resurrection. The apostle Paul says in 1 Cor 15:12–15:

> But if it is preached that Christ has been raised from the dead, how can some of you say that there is no resurrection of the dead? If there is no resurrection of the dead, then not even Christ has been raised. And if Christ has not been raised, our preaching is useless and so is your faith. More than that, we are then found to be false witnesses about God, for we have testified about God that he raised Christ from the dead.

In this passage we see the centrality of the resurrection for Christian belief. Paul says that if Jesus has not been raised, "our preaching is useless, and so is your faith." A Christianity without the resurrection is no Christianity at all, since the hope of eternal life for Christians is based on Jesus' resurrection. Paul then goes on to say that he would be a "false witness" if Jesus had not been raised. Thus, Christianity stands or falls on the resurrection.

Did Jesus really rise from the dead? Can a rational person believe in something so fantastic? What role can history play, and how would we know, historically speaking, whether Jesus actually rose from the dead? William Lane Craig and N.T. Wright are two scholars who have recently offered the strongest arguments for the resurrection.[9] For the most part, we will outline Craig's arguments here.

In order to make his case, Craig uses what are called the "criteria of authenticity" that many scholars, both skeptical and conservative, use in their studies of the Gospels.[10] These criteria do not assume that the Bible is God's word, or that it is inspired or inerrant. Such an argument for the historicity

---

9. For a summary of Craig's arguments on the resurrection, see Craig, *Reasonable Faith*, 333–404. For his scholarly defense, see Craig, *Assessing the New Testament Evidence*. For Wright's scholarly defense, see his *Resurrection of the Son of God*.

10. See Craig, *Reasonable Faith*, 296–98, 395–96.

of the resurrection would be circular if it assumed the New Testament was God's word. Instead, the criteria, as Craig uses them, assume simply that the New Testament contains ancient documents that make historical claims, some of which may be accurate, some not. Such criteria can be used on any ancient document that claims to record historical events, to see whether each event recorded is likely to be authentic.

The criteria, correctly used, can demonstrate a higher probability that events a document records are actually historical. For example, the *criterion of independent, early attestation* assumes that, if an event is attested to by multiple early and independent sources, it is likely to be authentic. The *criterion of embarrassment* assumes that, if an event is embarrassing to the author of a text, or it doesn't fit with the argument the author is making, it is unlikely to have been fabricated. For example, in Mark 13:32, speaking of the day of judgment, Jesus says, "No one knows about that day or hour, not even the angels in heaven, nor the Son, but only the Father." If Jesus is God, how could he not know when the day of judgment is coming? Since this verse doesn't fit well with the doctrine of Jesus' divinity, it is unlikely to have been fabricated. Finally, the criterion of *Semitisms* assumes that if a NT source has "Aramaic or Hebraic forms" it is more likely to be authentic. Since the NT was written in Greek, and Jesus and the early disciples spoke Aramaic, then Aramaic (or Hebrew) underpinnings of a phrase in Greek would mean the Greek phrase is based on an earlier, more primitive phrase, and thus more likely to be authentic.[11]

Many scholars have pointed out that often in historical Jesus studies, these criteria are misused. Skeptical scholars often assume that if an event or saying in the Gospels does not meet one or more of the criteria of authenticity, then it must be false. But logically, lack of evidence cannot prove a positive conclusion. In other words, simply because a report in the NT doesn't meet a criterion for authenticity, it doesn't follow that it is false. It could not meet the criterion and still be true. The criteria cannot rule out an event as historical, they can only show, positively, that an event is *more likely* to be historical. Basically, the criteria are *sufficient* to demonstrate historicity, but not *necessary*.[12]

Regarding the Gospels, what is not widely appreciated is that the Gospel writers researched and used earlier sources to write their accounts of

---

11. Craig, *Reasonable Faith*, 298.

12. See Craig, *Reasonable Faith*, 290–98; Komoszewski et al., *Reinventing Jesus*, 39–52; and Evans, *Fabricating Jesus*, 19–33, 46–51.

Jesus' life.[13] For example, Mark used earlier, primitive sources to describe the passion story, the last days of Jesus' life.[14] Some material in Matthew and Luke is word-for-word identical in the Greek, which means they used a common source to report these events which scholars call "Q." Then Matthew had sources the other Gospel writers did not have, and Luke had sources the others didn't have. This means Matthew and Luke used four sources to write their Gospels: They used Mark, Q, the "Matthean" source, and the "Lukan" source.[15] Therefore, we can discover primitive, early sources the Gospel writers used which predate the writing of the Gospels themselves. Ed Komoszewski calls these "the Gospel behind the Gospels."[16] The more primitive these sources are, the stronger the argument is that they are historical.

Craig goes on to make his case for the resurrection, based on the sources used in the New Testament. He argues that the resurrection is the inference to the best explanation for the data in the New Testament. That is, given the NT evidence, Jesus' literal resurrection is more likely to have taken place than any of the alternative explanations. Again, all Craig assumes for his argument is that the New Testament contains the earliest documents we have that claim to report the actual events in Jesus' life.

Interestingly, the earliest account of Jesus' resurrection in the New Testament is not in the Gospels, but in 1 Cor 15:3–8:

> For what I received I passed on to you as of first importance: that Christ died for our sins according to the Scriptures, that he was buried, that he was raised on the third day according to the Scriptures, and that he appeared to Peter, and then to the Twelve. After that, he appeared to more than five hundred of the brothers and sisters at the same time, most of whom are still living, though some have fallen asleep. Then he appeared to James, then to all the apostles, and last of all he appeared to me also . . .

Scholars have pointed out that this is likely an ancient creed that would have been recited in early church meetings. It predates the writing

---

13. For a theory on the inspiration of Scripture which reconciles God's inspiration with the writers' disparate styles and research, see Craig, "Men Moved by the Holy Spirit," 45–82.

14. Craig, *Reasonable Faith*, 362.

15. See Komoszewski et al., *Reinventing Jesus*, 22–25. For a detailed discussion, see Stein, *Synoptic Problem*.

16. Komoszewski, et al., *Reinventing Jesus*, 21–31.

of 1 Corinthians, which was one of Paul's earliest letters to begin with.[17] We know Paul is quoting a creed here because of some of the *Semitisms*. "Received" and "passed on" are technical, rabbinic terms based on underlying Hebrew words that rabbis used to describe how their teaching should be passed on to others. The term for "Peter" in this passage is actually "Cephas," the Aramaic term for "Peter." And there are other primitive, non-Pauline terms here as well, such as "the twelve," "the third day," and "he was raised." It also has a structure and cadence to it which means it was likely memorized. Therefore, this passage passes the *Semitisms* test for an early source.[18] Craig notes the significance: "Paul probably received this tradition no later than his visit to Jerusalem in AD 36 (Gal 1:18), if not earlier in Damascus. It thus goes back to within the first five years after Jesus' death."[19] This is important. It means that the early church was memorizing a saying about Jesus' resurrection in the first few years after his death. The resurrection, then, was not a legend or myth that Christians added later to convince people that Jesus was the Messiah. It was believed right from the beginning of the Christian movement.

Thus, Craig makes his case for the resurrection based on three well-attested New Testament facts: (1) the empty tomb, (2) the resurrection appearances, and (3) the origins of Christianity. Let's take these one at a time.

First, the reports of the empty tomb are based on some of the earliest and most primitive sources in the NT. Craig notes that Paul's creed above presupposes the empty tomb, since it says "he was buried" and "he was raised." In first-century Judaism, there was no concept of people "living on" after their death without their bodies rising. The idea of someone living on in our memory is a modern concept (which Dr. McCoy references at the end of *Star Trek II* about Spock: "He's really not dead as long as we remember him.") Since there was no concept like this in first-century Judaism, the empty tomb is presupposed by Paul's creed. As well, the phrase, "the third day" in the creed presupposes an empty tomb. Why would the first Christians believe that Jesus was raised on the "third day" (since, of course, they were not present to actually witness the resurrection)? Likely because it was

---

17. The scholarly consensus is that 1 Corinthians dates to between AD 53–57. See Thiselton, *First Epistle*, 31–32.

18. For a quick summary of the creed, see Strobel, *Case for Christ*, 249–52. For technical studies of the creed, see Craig, *Assessing the New Testament*, 1–49; and Wright, *Resurrection*, 317–29.

19. Craig, *Reasonable Faith*, 362.

the third day when the empty tomb was discovered. Therefore, the earliest source for the resurrection in the NT, 1 Cor 15, assumes an empty tomb.[20]

Paul's creed also compares well with the passion narrative in Mark. Many scholars believe that Mark's passion story is based on extremely early eyewitness accounts that date to within seven years of Jesus' crucifixion.[21] Craig then argues that Mark's passion narrative also includes the empty tomb narrative.[22] Thus, we have two *early and independent* sources for the empty tomb.

Finally, Matthew, Luke, and John all use independent sources for their empty tomb narratives. N.T. Wright examines the features of each of these three Gospel accounts and concludes that each account is based on early reports of the resurrection.[23] Matthew's account has "traces of prior tradition in the non-Matthean vocabulary of his narrative," and it includes the story of the guard at the tomb, which the other Gospels don't report, Craig declares.[24] Luke's source for his narrative is also independent since he relates the disciples going to the tomb to confirm the women's account (and this story was not fabricated because it is independently confirmed in John).[25] John is so different from the other Gospels that it also counts as an independent source. Thus, we have four independent sources for the empty tomb in the Gospels. Craig points out that when historians find *two* independent sources for an event, they are ecstatic. But here we have *multiple* independent sources. All this means that the empty tomb narrative meets the criteria for *independent* and *early attestation*, which makes it highly likely to be historical.[26]

As well, there are multiple independent, early sources for the fact that the women discovered the empty tomb, as Wright points out.[27] This meets the *embarrassment criterion* because women were looked down upon in Jewish society and not thought to be credible witnesses. If the empty tomb story were fabricated, it is highly unlikely it would include women finding

---

20. Craig, *Reasonable Faith*, 361, 365.
21. Craig, *Reasonable Faith*, 362.
22. Craig, *Reasonable Faith*, 364.
23. See Wright, *Resurrection*, 587–615, especially 610–15.
24. Craig, *Reasonable Faith*, 365–66.
25. Craig, *Reasonable Faith*, 366.
26. See Craig, *Reasonable Faith*, 362–67. For the scholarly argument, see Craig, *Assessing the New Testament*, 85–115, 163–247.
27. Wright, *Resurrection*, 607–8.

the empty tomb instead of men. Therefore, it's almost certain that women did in fact find the tomb empty.[28]

For the second part of Craig's argument, he discusses the resurrection appearances, which also are attested by early and independent sources. Paul's creed lists several: Jesus "appeared to Peter, then to the Twelve," and then "to five hundred." He goes on to say Jesus appeared to James and to Paul himself. Jesus' appearance to Peter is confirmed by Luke's early source in Luke 24:34. Jesus' appearances to the twelve apostles are confirmed by independent sources in Luke 24:36–42 and John 20:19–20. The passage in John has the disciples feeling Jesus' wounds, which speaks to a *bodily* resurrection.[29] And the appearance to James, Jesus' brother, is fascinating because none of Jesus' siblings believed he was the Messiah while he was alive (Mark 3:21, 31–35, John 7:1–10). But in Acts, James is one of the key leaders in the early church, which likely means he was converted after Jesus died, when Jesus appeared to him as Paul notes here. This is significant because it shows a skeptic being converted through a resurrection appearance.[30] Even Hans Grass, a skeptical scholar, admits that James' conversion is strong evidence for the resurrection.[31] As well, since Paul speaks of his own experience seeing Jesus on the road to Damascus multiple times in his letters, and it is recounted three times in Acts, we have independent sources for the appearance to Paul as well. Just like James, Paul was a skeptic when Jesus appeared to him. This means we have independent sources that strongly imply two skeptics were converted by resurrection appearances. Therefore we have multiple sources, many of which are early, for the resurrection appearances.[32]

For the third part of Craig's argument, he demonstrates that the origin of Christianity is highly unlikely without the resurrection. Even skeptical scholars admit that the early Christians *believed* in the resurrection.[33] And since it was such a pillar of Christian thought, it is unthinkable Christianity would have begun without it. We have already seen Paul's quote above that without the resurrection, "our preaching is useless and so is your faith."

---

28. Wright, *Resurrection*, 607–8; and Craig, *Reasonable Faith*, 367–69.
29. See Craig, *Reasonable Faith*, 377–87.
30. Craig, *Reasonable Faith*, 379–80.
31. Craig, *Reasonable Faith*, 380.
32. Craig, *Reasonable Faith*, 377–87; and Craig, *Assessing the New Testament*, 51–84.
33. Craig, *Assessing the New Testament*, 405.

SECTION IV: MESSIANIC THEMES IN *TREK*

And we have seen that in Paul's creed in 1 Corinthians, belief in the resurrection was at the very beginning of the Christian movement.

The question is: How did belief in Jesus' resurrection come about? In the Jewish thought of the first century, the idea of a killed or crucified messiah was unthinkable. So was a resurrected messiah. The messiah was supposed to be a descendent of David and a conquering hero who would throw off the yoke of Rome and become king over Israel. It was unthinkable that the messiah could be crucified and still be the messiah, since he was supposed to reign forever.[34] Craig notes: "It is difficult to overemphasize what a disaster the crucifixion was for the disciples' faith. Jesus' death on the cross spelled a humiliating end for any hopes they had entertained that he was the Messiah."[35] In fact, the way that Rome got rid of Jewish rebels calling themselves messiahs was to crucify them. Once the messiah was dead, their movement was over. As well, there was no expectation in Jewish thought of a resurrection before the end of the world at the day of judgment. Instead, it was believed that, in the last days, everyone would be resurrected simultaneously. As Wright points out, since there was no expectation the Messiah would die and rise, the disciples certainly wouldn't have fabricated the story in order to prove Jesus was the Messiah to their Jewish friends and colleagues.[36]

Some scholars have maintained that the early Christians got the idea for a resurrected messiah from pagan myths of dying and rising gods, but this is highly unlikely. For one thing, Jews in Palestine at the time detested pagan beliefs and practices. The disciples would not have wanted to be seen copying pagan beliefs in order to convince their Jewish friends of Jesus' resurrection.[37] In fact, Martin Hengel argues that because there was a belief in a resurrection at the end of time among first-century Jews in Palestine, pagan religions could not get a foothold in that area.[38] And while some scholars have found parallels to Jesus' resurrection in pagan myths, the parallels are a stretch and often exaggerated. In one common example, the Osiris myth, Osiris is cut up into fourteen pieces and somehow cobbled back together and brought back to life, but one piece of Osiris is missing. It's then unclear whether Osiris is brought back to

---

34. Craig, *Assessing the New Testament*, 406.
35. Craig, *Reasonable Faith*, 388.
36. See Wright, *Resurrection*, 205–6, 686; and Craig, *Reasonable Faith*, 392–94.
37. Nash, *Gospel and the Greeks*, 184.
38. Craig, *Reasonable Faith*, 391.

life *on earth*, and seen by others, or is simply a god of the underworld. This is a far cry from Jesus' bodily resurrection.[39] In fact, some of the parallels between pagan myths and Christianity date to later centuries, meaning that it is more likely pagan religions borrowed from Christian ideas rather than the other way around.[40] For example, Rudolph Bultmann famously argued that many Gospel resurrection accounts were based on earlier Gnostic myths and sources. However, the evidence for these Gnostic sources postdates the writing of the New Testament.[41] Thus, there are no religious beliefs, Jewish or pagan, which can explain the early Christians' belief in the resurrection. The messiah wasn't supposed to die and be raised, and the likelihood that Jewish Christians in Palestine borrowed from pagan thought is ridiculously small.

Given the New Testament facts about the empty tomb, the resurrection appearances, and the origins of Christianity, New Testament scholars who do not believe in the resurrection have had a difficult time explaining how early Christians came to believe in it and preach it. Many theories have been proposed over the years, from the idea that the disciples stole the body, to perhaps Jesus simply swooning on the cross and not actually dying, to the disciples going to the wrong tomb, to hallucinations the disciples may have had of Jesus after he died. But all of these theories strain credulity, given the early and independent narratives we have of Jesus' death and resurrection in the NT. Some theories, such as the hallucination theory, are hard to believe given that five hundred people saw Jesus at the same time. How could five hundred people have the same hallucination simultaneously? Other theories, like the idea that Jesus didn't die on the cross but fainted, even though he was stabbed with a Roman sword to make sure he was dead, are also nearly impossible to believe.[42]

Thus, Craig concludes, the resurrection of Jesus is the inference to the best explanation. It is the most likely explanation compared to other theories, given the facts we have seen in the New Testament.

This brings us back to Spock's sacrifice and his resurrection. We saw that Spock sacrificed his life to save the *Enterprise* crew and was then resurrected on the Genesis Planet. Given what the Genesis Device could do, it

---

39. Komoszewski et al., *Reinventing Jesus*, 251.
40. Nash, *Gospel and the Greeks*, 187.
41. Yamauchi, *Pre-Christian Gnosticism*, 163–86.
42. See Craig's analysis of these theories in *Reasonable Faith*, 371–95.

was rational to believe that Spock had come back to life. And given what an all-powerful God can do, it is rational to believe that he brought Jesus back to life as well.

SECTION V

Paradise in *Trek*

INTRODUCTION: "ET IN ARCADIA EGO, PART 2" (*PICARD*)

NUMEROUS *STAR TREK* STORIES explore the idea of paradise and the human condition. Are humans fit for paradise? Can we flourish in a paradise if it has no challenges, no pain or fear, and we live there forever? Wouldn't we get bored when we run out of things to do? Would we grow tired of living with no hurdles to overcome? From *The Original Series* to the latest *Trek* iterations, paradise is not a place where humans can flourish.

Recently, in the *Picard* episode "Et in Arcadia Ego, Part 2," Captain Picard dies and goes to the afterlife where he meets Data, who tells him the afterlife is "a massively complex quantum simulation." Data's memories are stored in a quantum computer, and this consists of the afterlife he's experiencing. He tells Picard that Picard has to go back to the land of the living. Data requests that Picard pull the plug on his memories, thus ending Data's existence in the afterlife. Data maintains that "mortality gives meaning to human life . . . a butterfly that lives forever is not really a butterfly at all." But is this really the case? Living forever is only meaningless if there are no meaningful tasks to accomplish, or the joy there dissipates over time.

As we will see next with the *Star Trek* film *Generations*, there are numerous reasons why heaven will be unimaginably exciting and joyful. With endless adventures to pursue, infinite exploration into God's beautiful essence, deep explorations into each other's souls, and work to be

SECTION V: PARADISE IN *TREK*

accomplished there, heaven will be completely fulfilling for us as human beings. In *Generations*, Kirk and Picard end up in a paradise called "the Nexus" and conclude that it isn't a place where humans can flourish because there are no challenges there. But as we will see, the Nexus isn't heaven.

In the TOS episode "Return of the Archons," we explore an *inner* paradise, a joyful and peaceful state of mind. In this episode, "joy, peace, and tranquility" can only come from the brutal control of a being called Landru, resulting in a mindless contentment. We will see that this is a stereotype of the actual joy, peace, and love Christians can experience in this life through surrender to God's authority in the Spirit-filled life. Paradoxically and incredibly, true spiritual freedom to flourish as humans comes from being servants of God.

11

Heaven: An Illusory Happiness?
Star Trek Generations Film
(Original Series and Next Generation)

WATCH *STAR TREK GENERATIONS* (1994 FILM)

IN THE STAR TREK film *Generations*, Captains Picard and Kirk team up to defeat Soran, an evil genius who is trying very hard to get back into the "Nexus," an energy ribbon which is a doorway into paradise. The story begins as Kirk appears to die of a blast from the energy ribbon while he is a visitor on a training mission for the new *Enterprise*-B flagship. Attempting to help the crew save several Federation vessels from being destroyed by the mysterious ribbon, Kirk disappears when the ribbon slices a chunk out of the *Enterprise*'s secondary hull. He is missing and presumed dead, but dozens of Federation passengers from the doomed vessels are beamed to safety, including, we find out later, the scientist Soran.

Seventy-eight years later, Captain Picard and *Enterprise*-D are also called to an emergency regarding the mysterious ribbon. A star is being destroyed nearby, which would kill millions of people on nearby planets. Soran, who is still alive these years later, is trying to get back inside the Nexus by destroying the star, which would change the gravity of its solar system and bring the Nexus right to him. Guinan, who has been inside the Nexus before, warns Picard that if he finds himself in it, he will never want

SECTION V: PARADISE IN *TREK*

to leave because the "joy" he will feel in the Nexus is overwhelming. Clearly, Soran has become obsessed and dangerous, trying to get back inside the Nexus.

Picard beams down to Soran's planet but is unable to stop him from destroying the star. The Nexus then envelops the planet, transferring Picard into the Nexus. While Picard experiences intense joy in the Nexus, he realizes it isn't real when he sees a miniature star, the star that was just destroyed, exploding over and over again in a tiny Christmas ornament, part of a holiday scene he experiences there. He decides he needs to get out of the Nexus to try and stop Soran, but he needs some help. Guinan appears (an echo of her that remained in the Nexus). She tells Picard that time has no meaning in the Nexus, which means that he can leave it whenever he wants and go to any time in history (or the future) that he desires. She also tells him that James Kirk is in the Nexus, and for Kirk, it's as if he's just arrived there as well. Picard goes to find Kirk to help him stop Soran. Kirk doesn't want to help Picard at first, but when he relives one of his favorite things—jumping a ravine on his favorite horse—it no longer means anything to him because he doesn't feel any fear. Since it isn't dangerous to do, it doesn't pose a challenge for him. The Nexus isn't real, and it's not a place for humans to flourish. The two captains leave the Nexus together, and they go back in time to immediately before Soran destroys the star. They are successful in stopping Soran, but Kirk dies in the battle. His sacrifice is not in vain because millions of lives from nearby planets are spared.

WORLDVIEW ANALYSIS

This film, like a lot of *Star Trek* stories before it, raises the issue of what heaven will be like. If it's a paradise with no fear and no challenges to overcome, how can humans really flourish there?

> GUINAN: The energy ribbon [is] a doorway to another place that we call the Nexus . . . It was like being inside joy. As if joy was something tangible . . . and you could wrap yourself in it like a blanket. And never in my entire life have I been as content . . .
>
> [TO PICARD]: If you go, you're not going to care about anything. Not this ship, Soran, nothing. All you'll want is to stay in the Nexus.

Here Guinan describes the Nexus as the ultimate paradise, a place where unspeakable joy envelops a person. Her language here is similar to descriptions of the joy of heaven in the Bible. For example, Ps 16:11 says, "You will fill me with joy in your presence, with eternal pleasures at your right hand." And Revelation describes the eternal state, the new heaven and new earth, this way: "[God] will wipe every tear from their eyes. There will be no more death or mourning or crying or pain, for the old order of things has passed away" (Rev 21:4).

We later learn that anyone in the Nexus can relive any part of their lives over again (unlike heaven). How many of us would like a do-over for something in our lives that we didn't get right the first time? When Picard enters the Nexus, he is celebrating Christmas with a wife and children he never had but he'd always wanted. He is transfixed. And Kirk is allowed to relive the day he asked Antonia to marry him. Guinan has told Picard that once he's in the Nexus he will never want to leave. And yet, both Picard and Kirk decide to leave relatively quickly. Why?

> KIRK: I must have jumped that fifty times. Scared the hell out of me. Except this time . . . Because it isn't real. [Kirk sees a woman on a horse on a distant hill]
>
> PICARD: Antonia?
>
> KIRK: She isn't real either is she? Nothing here is . . . Nothing here matters.

Here we see that Kirk is dissatisfied with the Nexus because he realizes it isn't real. When he doesn't feel fear, he realizes he's not actually in danger, thus there is no risk or challenge here. He decides to leave and help Picard defeat Soran. Likewise, although Picard is enraptured by the Nexus at first, he sees a hologram of the Veridian star, the star which Soran destroyed, continuously exploding in a small Christmas ornament on the tree in his Nexus home. He is reminded of the tragedy that befell the solar system he was unable to save, and he realizes the Nexus isn't real. He decides to leave as well.

REALITY AND MEANING IN THE HOLODECK

Can a virtual reality experience be truly meaningful? In *The Next Generation*, the holodeck is a large room on the *Enterprise* which projects holograms to create an incredibly realistic virtual environment. It uses various transporter and forcefield technologies to create "holomatter," which means that persons and objects in the holodeck feel like solid, genuine objects.

Section V: Paradise in *Trek*

In "Why Not Live in the Holodeck?" Philip Tallon and Jerry Walls argue that living out scenarios in the holodeck is not satisfying because it is not real life.[1] To support this claim they describe Aristotle as maintaining that "a beautiful object needs more than an 'orderly arrangement of parts'; it also needs 'magnitude,'" which they describe as a "reversal of fortune" in a story. In other words, real peril and real danger.[2] But why is real peril necessary to enjoy an adventure? All kinds of adventures can be played out in the holodeck, including real challenges, climaxes, and denouements in holodeck stories, with *simulations* of danger. The fact is our hearts often beat faster with anxiety when we are merely *watching* the climax of a movie or a stressful scene. For example, in one study scientists measured breathing, heartbeat, and blood pressure while participants watched a stressful five-minute scene from a movie. They found the increased heart rate, breathing, and blood pressure were brought about by *emotional stress*. They warn that people with weak hearts should not watch such movies.[3] But the use of holomatter in the holodeck means the simulations there are much more real than in the movies. Persons and objects feel as solid as they do in real life. The idea that Kirk wouldn't feel fear in the Nexus simply because it was a simulation is not borne out by the science. In a simulation this true to life, his heartbeat and blood pressure would certainly rise. Psychologically, since he had always felt fear before when he jumped the ravine, it is almost certain he would have felt it again.

Psychologists are now beginning to use virtual reality therapy to treat anxiety disorders precisely for this reason. Psychological treatment for anxiety has always included imagining the fearful situation, mentally *reentering* the place where the anxiety began, and then overcoming it. This works because imagining the former situation usually brings on the original anxiety. Studies are beginning to show that virtual reality therapy can help anxiety disorders and other disorders precisely *because* it can simulate the fearful situation. Patients can reenter their fear in a safe environment and then overcome it.[4] It is almost certain, then, that Kirk would have felt the same fear in the simulation because he had been conditioned to feel fear whenever he jumped.

1. Tallon and Walls, "Why Not Live in the Holodeck?," 161–72.
2. Tallon and Walls, "Why Not Live in the Holodeck?," 166.
3. Rothman, "Intense Movies," paras. 2–4.
4. See Maples-Keller et al., "Use of Virtual Reality," 103–13.

Heaven: An Illusory Happiness?

When discussing the Nexus, Tallon and Walls go on to quote Richard Swinburne, who relates that if one has no personal responsibility for others in a possible world, it is ultimately unsatisfying.[5] For example, Tallon and Walls argue that while danger can be simulated in the holodeck, since the other characters in the simulation aren't real and they cannot feel real pain or disappointment, leading them in an adventure is unfulfilling. But there are two problems with this. First, in his book Swinburne is not arguing against responsibility in virtual reality in general, he is arguing against a world in which God deceives us, making it *appear* as if we have responsibility over others with real consequences when actually we do not.[6] But a holodeck is a simulation in which people freely choose to participate. True, the responsibility over others isn't the same in a simulation. We still know, in the back of our minds, that it is just a game, and it makes no difference in the real world. One reason for this is that we know we have to return to the real world. But simulations in the holodeck are so realistic, it would be easier than ever to forget that they are *not* the real world. Imagine that you could be in a simulation in which you could touch everything and everyone in it, and they felt just as real as objects in the real world. That's what the holodeck is (and presumably, the Nexus). After finding or designing a favorite simulation, why would you ever want to leave? The fact that some people have literally died playing video games because they wouldn't stop for a break for several days shows how addicting virtual reality can be.[7] As well, why can't people live a vicarious adventure without responsibility and still be caught up in it? Every weekend diehard football fans live vicarious adventures watching their favorite teams compete—teams for which they have literally no responsibility. But the excitement in watching is precisely because it feels as if they are in some way competing themselves. Of course, they would not have the *same* satisfaction as a player on the field who had practiced for months. But if watching a game is unsatisfying, why are billions of dollars spent on spectator sports every year? Tallon and Walls' argument falls flat.

Also, when comparing the Nexus or the holodeck to heaven, an important factor is that, even though in the holodeck responsibility for others is simulated, in heaven responsibility for others is real. Verses such as 2 Tim 2:12 indicate God's redeemed people will reign in heaven: "If we endure,

---

5. Swinburne, *Providence and the Problem of Evil*, 147.
6. Swinburne, *Providence and the Problem of Evil*, 140–41.
7. Kuperczko et al., "Sudden Gamer Death," abstract, paras. 1–5.

we will also reign with him." Revelation also indicates God's people will reign in the future "on the earth" (Rev 5:10).[8] And as we will see below, there are kings who rule over their different peoples and cultures in heaven. Heaven is no simulation. We will have real bodies, real leadership, and real responsibility.

Finally, one of the reasons Picard and Kirk sense the Nexus is unreal is because of glitches in the system. Picard sees the exploding Veridian star in a Christmas ornament, reminding him that he's in a simulation. And Kirk walks through a door to his former bedroom, only to find himself in his old barn, not his bedroom at all, which reminds him that he too, is in a simulation. The Nexus has glitches, but heaven does not. As we will see below, heaven is more real and concrete than life on earth is.

BIBLICAL DESCRIPTIONS OF HEAVEN

Heaven is going to be an amazing place because we will see God directly for the first time. We will be overwhelmed with the love, joy, and beauty of the Trinity: Father, Son, and Holy Spirit. King David once said that he wanted to "gaze upon the beauty of the Lord," and we will be able to do this in heaven, according to 1 John 3, because "We shall be like him, for we shall see him as he is" (Ps 27:4 and 1 John 3:2). This clear sight of God and the beauty of his attributes is what Thomas Aquinas called the "beatific vision," and we will explore it in more detail below.

Does this mean that heaven is merely an ethereal existence? Is heaven a place only in the mind but not experienced by the body? One of the reasons people sometimes give that they don't look forward to heaven is that they have a mystical view in which we will do nothing but float on clouds and play harps. But the Bible indicates heaven is at least partially a physical existence in a new earth:

> Then I saw a *"new heaven and a new earth,"* for the first heaven and the first earth had passed away, and there was no longer any sea. I saw the Holy City, the new Jerusalem, coming down out of heaven from God . . . (Rev 21:1–2, emphasis mine)[9]

Here God creates a new heaven and earth, and places us in and near the new Jerusalem, which indicates some type of physical existence. The

---

8. See also Rev 20:4–6, Dan 7:27, and 1 Cor 6:1–3.
9. See also Isa 65:17, 66:22, and 2 Pet 3:13.

Heaven: An Illusory Happiness?

Bible asserts that we will have resurrected bodies that are like Jesus' resurrected body: "The Lord Jesus Christ . . . will transform our lowly bodies so that they will be like his glorious body" (Phil 3:20–21). Jesus had a resurrected body that people could touch, and he ate meals with his disciples (John 20:24–29, 21:1–14). Even though at times people who knew him didn't recognize him (Luke 24:31), and he could seem to appear and disappear at will in different locations (John 20:14–16), he still had some type of physical existence with which people could interact. There is, of course, a lot we don't know about what our bodies will be like in heaven—what exactly is a "glorious body"? A body that has its own light? That's certainly possible. As we will see in volume 2, in a discussion of the *Voyager* episode "Cathexis," some people who have near-death experiences see their loved ones or friends with shining bodies in heaven. What we know for sure is that because Jesus interacted physically with his environment, we will also interact physically with ours.[10]

As well, when we explore the garden of Eden in volume 2, in a discussion of the TOS episode "The Apple," we will see that there was work to do in Eden before the fall. Because there was work in Eden and heaven restores (much) of what we lost in Eden, it is likely we will have work to do in heaven as well—work that we are uniquely designed to do, the results of which will last forever. Rev 21 says of the new Jerusalem:

> The nations will walk by its light [the glory of God], and the kings of the earth will bring their splendor into [the city]. On no day will its gates ever be shut, for there will be no night there. The glory and honor of the nations will be brought into it. (Rev 21:24–25)

"Splendor" here can be translated as "glory" or "honor." As Andy Crouch points out,[11] this description is partially a quotation of Isa 60:11, which says, "People may bring you the wealth of the nations—their kings led in triumphal procession."[12] Like Rev 21, Isa 60 says that the sun and moon will no longer be necessary, "for the Lord will be your everlasting light" (Isa 60:19). This means that Isaiah is also talking about the eternal city, not just God's temple on earth. This is undoubtedly why John quotes Isa 60 in his passage about the new Jerusalem. Richard Mouw speculates

---

10. See Wright, *Resurrection*, for the debate on the nature of Jesus' resurrected body and a defense of his body as *physically* resurrected.

11. Crouch, *Culture Making*, 166–67.

12. See also Isa 60:6–7, 9, 13.

about what this might mean for culture, the new creation, and how they go together:

> The contents of the City will be more akin to our present cultural patterns than is usually acknowledged in discussions of the afterlife. Isaiah pictures the Holy City as a center of commerce, a place that receives the vessels, goods, and currency of commercial activity.[13]

As Crouch points out, in Isaiah's procession kings bring things that are culturally valuable to them, such as gold and frankincense, to worship God and lay them at his feet. God says of them: "They will be accepted as offerings on my altar, and I will adorn my glorious temple" (Isa 60:7). Some of these artifacts come from different ethnicities and cultures. "Just as the king of a nation, in the biblical mind, is the representative of an entire *ethnos* or people, the glory of a nation is simply its greatest and most distinctive cultural achievements [and cultural goods]," Crouch says.[14] Thus, the "glory and honor" of the nations (*ethnos*) in Rev 21 are these cultural goods that will be used to worship God. Surprisingly, it seems as if *work*, done in heaven, will be required to make such beautiful artifacts, glorifying God from different peoples. If heaven is a place where we will fully flourish using the gifts God has given us, then it will be people who are gifted in making such artifacts who will fashion them.

What else do we know about heaven? Well, Jesus promises to create a unique place for each of us in heaven: "In my Father's house are many rooms; if that were not so, would I have told you that I am going there to prepare a place for you?" (John 14:2). We can only imagine what kind of place God will make for us, but it must surpass anything we could ever experience here on earth.

And because God is the center of our heavenly experience, we will experience him in new ways. His glory will illuminate the new Jerusalem: "I did not see a temple in the city, because the Lord God Almighty and the Lamb are its temple. The city does not need the sun or the moon to shine on it, for the glory of God gives it light, and the Lamb is its lamp" (Rev 21:22–23).[15] And we will have a new intimacy with God that we didn't have before: "God's dwelling place is now among the people, and he will dwell

---

13. Mouw, *When the Kings Come Marching In*, 20. For his extended argument, see 17–42.

14. Crouch, *Culture Making*, 167–68.

15. "The Lamb" is a metaphor for Jesus. See John 1:29.

with them. They will be his people, and God himself will be with them and be their God" (Rev 21:1–3). In other words, "Heaven is the place where God most fully makes known his presence to bless."[16]

We will also worship God in heaven:

> After this I looked and there before me was a great multitude that no one could count, from every nation, tribe, people and language, standing before the throne and before the Lamb . . . And they cried out in a loud voice: "Salvation belongs to our God, who sits on the throne, and to the Lamb.' (Rev 7:9–10)

This beautiful picture of worship in heaven confirms that people of all ethnicities and cultures will worship God, united as one before the Lamb. Verses such as Rev 4:8 suggest that worship of God will be continuous in heaven, although it is not clear whether *all* of heaven will worship the Lord all the time (and there may be many ways to worship him, including making the cultural artifacts discussed above).

To summarize, God will be the center of our experience in heaven, but there will also be a new physical earth, physically resurrected bodies, work, and the creation of cultural artifacts in heaven.

Regarding the beauty of heaven itself, biblical metaphors struggle to fully capture it. For example, some verses declare that the beauty of the new Jerusalem "was like that of a very precious jewel, like a jasper, clear as crystal," and "the city [was made of] . . . pure gold, as pure as glass" (Rev 21:11, 18). These descriptions are most likely metaphorical.[17] The new Jerusalem is also described as a square—as high as it is wide and long (Rev 21:16–17). Since the dimensions are perfect, they appear to be symbolic.[18] The point is that the new city will be overwhelmingly beautiful and perfect. And as we saw above, there will be no more pain or grief in heaven, but unspeakable joy in God's presence (on joy, see below).

WILL HEAVEN BE BORING?

So many *Trek* stories, including *Generations*, imply that a paradise (like heaven) will be boring because there are no challenges and no creativity

---

16. Grudem, *Systematic Theology*, 1159.

17. See Beale, *Revelation*, 1064–65. But Andy Crouch notes that gold can be hammered until it is translucent. See Crouch, *Culture Making*, 164–65.

18. See Beale, *Revelation*, 1073–78.

there.[19] But is that really the case? As we will see, our adventures in heaven will be greater than our adventures here on earth.

Is it wrong to imagine heaven? The Bible gives limited descriptions of life in heaven, so we can also use our imaginations, when based on Scripture, to make reasonable predictions of what heaven will be like. As Randy Alcorn points out, "We cannot anticipate or desire what we cannot imagine. That's why . . . God has given us glimpses of heaven in the Bible—to *fire up our imagination* and kindle our desire for heaven in our hearts."[20]

What thought-out predictions about heaven can we make? For one thing, there are rewards in heaven for our earthly life (Luke 6:23, Rev 22:12, Matt 16:27, 1 Cor 3:8, 11–14, among other verses). Because of these rewards, it is unlikely we will forget our lives on earth. How can we understand or enjoy receiving our rewards if we do not know why we received them? If we don't know why we received them, how could we lay them at Jesus' feet?[21] But since there are no tears or pain in heaven, how could we be aware of our trials, failures, sins, or grief in our earthly lives and not be full of sadness?

Here we will largely follow Peter Kreeft's arguments about why heaven is not boring in his book *Heaven: The Heart's Deepest Longing*. We will also explore some of C.S. Lewis' more beautiful and fascinating descriptions of heaven.

Kreeft argues that God knows our whole lives from beginning to end and will see us through his eyes of redemption: "Behold, you are all fair, my love. There is no spot or wrinkle in you."[22] Since we are swallowed up in eternity, we will see the meaning of all events as a whole.[23] And because God knows all of our lives, every failure, heartbreak, and sin, and how he redeemed them, using them for good, we will see our lives through his eyes. Thomas Howard describes this from God's perspective:

---

19. See for example, the TOS episodes "This Side of Paradise," "I, Mudd," The Apple" (see vol. 2, ch. 6), and "Return of the Archons" (see ch. 12).

20. Alcorn, *Heaven*, 16 (emphasis mine).

21. Since in Rev 4:10 the twenty-four elders lay their crowns at Jesus' feet, it is likely we will too.

22. Kreeft, *Heaven*, 86. A quotation from Song 4:7.

23. Kreeft, *Heaven*, 85–86. Here Kreeft uses Boethius' view of time, in which God *sees* all time, past, present, and future in one awareness. This is a problematic view. For a critique, see Craig, *Time and Eternity*, 79–216. However, since God can still know the future using his middle knowledge (see ch. 6), Kreeft's application still stands.

Heaven: An Illusory Happiness?

I announce to you redemption. Behold I make all things new. Behold I do what cannot be done. I restore the years that the locusts and worms have eaten. I restore the years which you have drooped away upon your crutches and in your wheelchair. I restore the symphonies and operas your deaf ears never heard, and the snowy massif your blind eyes have never seen, and the freedom lost to you through plunder, and the identity lost to you because of calumny and failure of justice; and I restore to you the good which your foolish mistakes have cheated you of. And I bring to you the Love of which all other loves speak, the Love which is joy and beauty, and which you have sought in a thousand streets and for which you have wept and clawed your pillow.[24]

Not only will we see our lives this way, but it makes sense that we will know *others* this deeply, through Jesus' eyes of redemption. We know there is community in heaven because we are all united in worshipping God there. What will our relationships in heaven be like? It is likely we will be filled with the joy of deeply knowing the lives of others and how they are redeemed as well. Kreeft notes that when we have reviewed our past life with "divine understanding and appreciation of every single experience ... we [will] milk all our meaning dry." Then we will do the same with others' lives, seeing them the way God sees them, "from within." We will know them "more intimately and completely than we could ever know our most intimate friend on earth because we share God's knowledge of each one."[25]

And if this is not enough, we will enjoy "exploration unto God" in heaven.[26] We will have eternity to explore God's unending knowledge, beauty, and goodness, finding ourselves lost in his loving light. As Kreeft points out, we think heaven will be boring because we do not understand *joy*. In our direct apprehension and enjoyment of God—the Beatific Vision—we will see God in his essence, as he really, deeply is. We will be overwhelmed by his love, his wisdom, the beauty of his attributes, and the eternal joy of the Trinity. The beatific vision is inspired by Paul's words in 1 Cor 13: "Now we see only a reflection as in a mirror; then we shall see face to face. Now I know in part; then I shall know fully, even as I am fully known" (1 Cor 13:12). Each one of us will enjoy God uniquely, as we were

---

24. Kreeft, *Heaven*, 87.

25. Kreeft, *Everything You Ever Wanted to Know*, 52. He links these ideas to purgatory, but purgatory is not mentioned in Scripture, and it is not necessary for his arguments here.

26. Kreeft, *Everything You Ever Wanted to Know*, 52.

uniquely made, because we were individually designed for the beatific vision in a way that fits with our nature.[27]

E.J. Fortman explains the beatific vision:

> What is the *essence of heaven?* . . . [It is the] beatific vision, love, and enjoyment of the triune God. For the three divine persons have an infinitely perfect vision and love and enjoyment of the divine essence and of one another. And in this infinite knowing, loving and enjoying lies the very life of the triune God, the very essence of their endless and infinite happiness. If the blessed are to be endlessly and supremely happy, then they must share in the very life of the triune God . . .[28]

What is this joy of heaven like? As we enjoy God's wisdom, which is "not just knowledge, but understanding," and his love, which is "not just liking," but *agape* love, God's self-giving love, we will be *overwhelmed* by God's joy. Wisdom and love "are the two things in our lives that are of heavenly substance, that are eternal, that are never boring, and that are stronger than death," Kreeft says.[29] Here he is worth quoting at length:

> Earth is God's beach, and when we are wise and loving, we are infants splashing happily in the wavelets of "that immortal sea." But when we are spiritually full grown . . . we will buoyantly plow [the sea's] breakers of wisdom and be borne up by its bottomless depths of love. Boredom, like pain, will be remembered as a joke when we are "drenched in joy."[30]

Kreeft goes on to say that "Heaven is not static or boring because it is not the end but the beginning, not the evening but the morning." It is like a new birth.[31] As C.S. Lewis wrote, all our adventures in this life pale in comparison with our adventures in the next. In his last book of *The Chronicles of Narnia* series, *The Last Battle*, Lewis hints at the amazing adventures to come. Here he describes the children at the end of their adventures in Narnia talking to Aslan, the great lion who is the Christ figure in the series:

---

27. On the beatific vision, see Zagzebski, "Heaven," 249–53.
28. Fortman, *Everlasting Life*, 309.
29. Both quotes are from Kreeft, *Heaven*, 95.
30. Kreeft, *Heaven*, 96. Here he quotes Wordsworth and C.S. Lewis, respectively.
31. Kreeft, *Heaven*, 94.

> [Aslan said:] "You do not yet look so happy as I mean you to be."
>
> Lucy said, "We're so afraid of being sent away, Aslan. And you have sent us back into our own world so often."
>
> "No fear of that," said Aslan. "Have you not guessed?"
>
> Their hearts leaped and a wild hope rose within them.
>
> "There *was* a real railway accident," said Aslan softly.
>
> "Your father and mother and all of you are—as you used to call it in the Shadow-Lands—dead. The term is over: the holidays have begun. The dream is ended: this is the morning."
>
> And as he spoke he no longer looked to them like a lion; but the things that began to happen after that were so great and beautiful that I cannot write them. And for us this is the end of all the stories, and we can most truly say that they all lived happily ever after. But for them it was only the beginning of the real story. All their life in this world and all their adventures in Narnia had only been the cover and the title page; now at last they were beginning Chapter One of the Great Story, which no one on earth has read, which goes on for ever, in which every chapter is better than the one before.[32]

Kreeft goes on to explain further reasons heaven is not boring. For example, is heaven a journey, or is it arriving at a destination? Some have argued that once you arrive at your destination, the fun has ended, so heaven must be an endless journey, an ever hoping for a destination but never arriving. But as Lewis points out, how could there be hope in the journey if there is no arriving at a satisfying destination?[33] Of course we will arrive at a destination in heaven, unimaginably wonderful (*and* we will have many journeys). But the reason why we arrive at destinations in this life and are disappointed is that we were made for another world. The arriving here is simply a taste that makes us thirsty for the next world. "There is something bigger than the world out there, hiding behind everything in the world, and our chief joy is with it. The world is a mask, and we must unmask it," Kreeft says. "We are outsiders, aliens, exiles. If only we could get *in!*"[34] He then quotes one of Lewis' famous essays on our longing for beauty:

> What more, you may ask, do we want? Ah, but we want so much more—something the books and aesthetics take little notice of . . . We do not merely want to see beauty, though, God knows,

32. Lewis, *Last Battle*, 228.
33. Kreeft, *Heaven*, 85.
34. Kreeft, *Heaven*, 111.

even that is bounty enough. We want something else which we can hardly put into words—to be united with the beauty we see, to pass into it, to receive it into ourselves, to bathe in it, to become part of it . . . At present we are on the outside of the world, the wrong side of the door. We discern the freshness and purity of morning, but they do not make us fresh and pure. We cannot mingle with the splendours we see. But all the leaves of the New Testament are rustling with the rumour that it will not always be so. Some day, God willing, we shall get *in*.[35]

In fact, Kreeft argues, one reason that we think the journey is better than the destination is that "we conceive of the end—truth, goodness, beauty, eternity, or heaven—as static and abstract rather than dynamic and concrete."[36] Life in heaven will be more "real" and substantial than this one, so the destination is infinitely more satisfying. Again, Lewis has a wonderful illustration of this in his allegory *The Great Divorce*. A spirit from heaven is trying to explain heaven to a ghost who is visiting:

"Will you come with me to the mountains?"
"I should require some assurances . . . an atmosphere of free inquiry . . ."
"No . . . no atmosphere of inquiry, for I will bring you to the land not of questions, but of answers, and you shall see the face of God."
"Ah, but . . . for me there is no such thing as a final answer . . . you must feel yourself that there is something stifling about the idea of finality . . . what is more soul destroying than stagnation?"
"You think that, because hitherto you have experienced truth only with the abstract intellect. I will bring you where you can taste it like honey and be embraced by it as if by a bridegroom. Your thirst will be quenched."[37]

Heaven's concreteness will be infinitely more satisfying than our current knowledge in the abstract.

What about our free will? How will we use our will in heaven? Kreeft notes that Aquinas makes a distinction between "two activities of the will: desiring an absent good and rejoicing in a present good. The latter is just as active as the former."[38] Here Kreeft describes this heavenly rejoicing:

35. Lewis, *Weight of Glory*, 37.
36. Kreeft, *Heaven*, 92.
37. Lewis, *Great Divorce*, 39–40.
38. Kreeft, *Heaven*, 93.

Heaven: An Illusory Happiness?

Thus, once Heaven is attained, the will does not rest in boredom. Nor does it work in frustration. *It rejoices in play.* Contemplation has traditionally been symbolized by play; divine Wisdom is pictured . . . as playing before God's face.[39]

. . .Work is like filling an empty pail; rest is like a full, quiet pool; play is like an *overflowing fountain.* Play . . . is not like climbing a mountain; it is like just walking or exploring or breathing or singing; better yet, it is *living*—you are quite happy never to come to the end.[40]

Of course, as Kreeft notes, on Earth play does eventually get boring and we want it to end. But that is because our play here involves *finite* objects, not infinite ones. Playing with infinite objects will never get boring because the exploration is unending.

Finally, it appears that some people who have had near-death experiences have left their bodies, gone to heaven, and then come back. We will explore reports of such experiences, why it is rational to believe at least some of them, and how they relate to heaven in volume 2.

Thus, the rich exploration of ourselves, others, and God in heaven, and the rejoicing in play there, make it a blissful place in which all our true human needs will be overwhelmingly fulfilled. So when Kirk and Picard reject the Nexus as a place of bliss where there is no challenge, and thus no humanity, they are rejecting a caricature of heaven rather than heaven itself. In the end, Kirk and Picard find a way to leave the Nexus, stop Soran, and save a solar system. But they didn't really find heaven. They found the Nexus.

---

39. Wisdom "rejoicing" in Prov 8:30–31 can mean "playing or frolicking like a child." See Koptak, *Proverbs*, 248.

40. These quotations are from Kreeft, *Heaven*, 93. (Some of the emphases are mine, some are his.)

12

Religion as the Opiate of the Masses?

"Return of the Archons" (*The Original Series*)

WATCH "RETURN OF THE ARCHONS" (TOS SEASON 1)

IN THIS EPISODE, SULU and another crew member from the *Enterprise* have beamed down to investigate a planet where another starship, called the *Archon*, went missing years ago. But they are both chased by the inhabitants of the planet. Before Sulu can beam out, he is hit with a ray from hooded figures who surround him. His personality changes to a smiling, vacuous peacefulness. When Kirk and crew beam down to investigate, they find the inhabitants of a medieval-looking town wearing a look of "mindless, vacant contentment," all walking in the same slow gait and greeting each other with "Joy to you." It becomes clear the landing party is in danger since they are not mindless and peaceful like the rest of the inhabitants. They witness someone who is "not of the body" killed by "The Lawgivers," hooded figures who enforce compliance.

The townspeople speak of "Landru," a person who gives them everything they need. Their minds are controlled by this Landru, who is seemingly omnipresent. He controls the population for "the good of the Body." Just before they are captured, Kirk and the others witness a projection of Landru on a wall. He is a middle-aged man dressed in a toga, and he declares: "You have come to a world without hate, without fear, without conflict . . . You will be absorbed . . . and in your submergence into the common being of the Body, you will find contentment and fulfillment. You will experience the absolute good." The landing party is then captured by the Lawgivers, and several are "absorbed" by the Body, losing their minds to vacant peacefulness. But Kirk is saved by an undercover villager who has not been absorbed and who helps them get their phasers and communicators back. The undercover villagers who help them call Kirk's crew "Archons," after the original Starfleet people who arrived there. Spock finally deduces that "Landru" is a supercomputer, created by a wise leader named Landru eons ago to lead the planet with wisdom and peace. But the Landru program became so controlling, the normal cultural development on the planet stagnated, and people who resisted his control lost their lives. Kirk and Spock are able to destroy the computer by catching it in a classic *Trek* contradiction: While Landru believes the Body must thrive in creativity, he has unwittingly destroyed that creativity with his control. As Kirk declares to Landru: "Without freedom of choice, there is no creativity. Without creativity, there is no life. The Body dies. The fault is yours." The computer is caught in the contradiction and overheats, destroying itself. Kirk tells the inhabitants they are now free to create their own lives.

WORLDVIEW ANALYSIS

> LAWGIVER: You attacked the Body. You have heard the Word and disobeyed. You will be absorbed . . . The Good is all. Landru is gentle. You will come.

Here we see Christian terminology such as "the body," "heard the word and disobeyed," and "lawgiver." Other terms used in the episode like "save," "blessed," and "joy, peace, and tranquility," link Christian ideas with the mind control of Landru. This mind control was likely a commentary on Christian hierarchy from the Middle Ages,[1] and we can see this with the medieval-looking robes of the "lawgivers" and the costumes and sets used

---

1. Pearson, "From Thwarted Gods," 19.

in the episode.[2] James Blish, who wrote short story adaptations of many of *The Original Series* episodes, often based his stories on earlier drafts of the scripts.[3] His adaptation of "Archons" uses the term "beatific" for the state McCoy is in after he is absorbed into the Body.[4] Thus, the "joy and peace" described in the episode are stereotypes of the beatific vision. We saw in chapter 11 that the beatific vision is a source of joy for those who go to heaven and can apprehend God and his essence directly. It is a distinctly Christian term, again linking the mind control here to Christianity. Note that here, "beatific" refers to an internal paradise, a (supposedly happy) mental state in which all who belong to Landru participate.

> McCOY: He goes to joy, peace, and tranquility. He goes to meet Landru. Happiness is to all of us, blessed by Landru.

Here we see McCoy absorbed into "the Body." He now has no mind of his own, and his "peace and tranquility" are only obtained through Landru's complete control. Thus, his "peace" consists of vacuous living and an empty mental life, something that no sane person would desire.

The show clearly implies that religious authority is a type of mind control which sucks the humanity out of all who are unfortunate enough to be absorbed by it. The enemy is the authority, who does not truly have the follower's good at heart. Certainly there are religious sects who control others in this way. But is this what actually happens to people who follow Jesus?

SPIRITUAL FREEDOM

The Bible describes two types of freedom. The first type of freedom is the ability to choose between good and evil, which God established in the garden of Eden. As we will see in volume 2, in our discussion of "The Apple" (TOS), God planted the "Tree of Knowledge" in the garden and told Adam and Eve they were not to eat of it, thus giving them a choice regarding whether they would obey or disobey him. This ability to choose was

---

2. Marc Cushman believes the story was a commentary on communist oppression during the Cold War, but the connection to Christian theology is hard to miss. See Cushman, *Voyages: TOS Season One*, 489.

3. Marc Cushman, email message to the author, January 2, 2024. See also Ketterer, *Imprisoned in a Tesseract*, 24–25, 249–50, 355.

4. Blish, *Star Trek: The Classic Episodes*, 220. Note that "Archons" was listed under Blish's name, but actually penned by his wife Judith Blish and her mother, Muriel Lawrence. See Ketterer, *Imprisoned in a Tesseract*, 25.

necessary for a love relationship with him. That is, if they had no choice in loving God, it would not truly be love on their part, and God wanted them to choose to genuinely love him.

The second kind of freedom, the most profound kind taught in the Scriptures, is spiritual freedom. Spiritual freedom is a paradox: The more we bow in surrender to God, the more we are truly free. It is surrendering to God's authority that makes us freer than we have ever been before.

Jesus said, "For whoever would save his life will lose it, but whoever loses his life for me will find it" (Matt 16:25). In another fascinating passage, Jesus dialogues with people who are considering becoming his followers and declares:

> "If you hold to my teaching, you are really my disciples. Then you will know the truth, and the truth will set you free." They answered him, "We are Abraham's descendants and have never been slaves of anyone. How can you say that we shall be set free?" Jesus replied, "I tell you the truth, everyone who sins is a slave to sin . . . So if the Son sets you free, you will be free indeed." (John 8:31–36)

The word "hold," as in "hold to my teaching," is the Greek word for "abide" or "remain." It has the connotation here of obeying the teaching, seeking to understand it better, persevering in it, and holding it as "precious."[5] That is, Jesus is saying here that once we obey and "hold" to his teaching, *then* we understand it and are set free. "Teaching" primarily refers to the gospel here, the good news that Jesus is the Messiah and he saves us from our sins. We are "set free" after we surrender to the truth of who Jesus is and his teachings. The Jewish leaders who were listening were taken aback at the implication that they were "slaves" and needed to be set free, because they believed that study of the Old Testament law set them free. But Jesus declares they are "slaves to sin" and only he, the Son, can set them free. Only in surrendering to Jesus' authority are we truly liberated. D.A. Carson summarizes: "True freedom is not the liberty to do anything we please, but the liberty to do what we ought; and it is genuine liberty because doing what we ought now pleases us."[6] How can this be? How can submission to Jesus' authority bring real freedom?

Recall that in chapter 4 we discussed virtue theory. According to Western virtue theory, which goes back to Plato and Aristotle, the right thing to do is what a virtuous person would do. A "virtue" is a habit or disposition

---

5. Carson, *Gospel According to John*, 348, emphasis mine.
6. Carson, *Gospel According to John*, 350.

that rightly allows the person to flourish according to their nature, or "essence." Their essence is a set of properties that makes them what they are. If a ball loses its roundness, it ceases to be a ball. Therefore, "roundness" is an *essential* property of a ball. It is a property that makes a ball what it is. In virtue theory, this set of properties, called an "essence," has an end purpose or goal, a reason for which it exists, which is the flourishing, or proper functioning of that thing. For example, a flourishing squirrel would be a squirrel that has a shiny coat and bushy tail and is able to gather food and reproduce. It flourishes according to its design.

As Christian thinkers incorporated virtue theory into their theology, acting virtuously fulfilled God's design for human beings and allowed them to *flourish* and to be "happy" or "blessed." Included is the idea that originally, God did not design humans to sin, so a "vice" does not allow a person to function and flourish as they were designed. Therefore, a vice takes away a person's "blessedness" or "happiness." We also saw that some habits, such as intellectual study, are virtues even if they aren't moral virtues, because they allow the person to flourish according to design. Therefore, since virtues allow a person to flourish, we are *more* human when we are virtuous, not less.

What does this have to do with freedom? According to Christian theology, a person is most free when they are flourishing according to their design; when they are acting "virtuously." According to Martensen:

> Only that existence can be called really free that lives and moves in full agreement with its proper being [its essence], that can unfold its powers unhindered and undisturbed.[7]

Evan Hopkins explains:

> And so in nature we say a creature is free when it can move in its own native element. The bird is free in the air, the fish in the water. Take either of them out of its element, and its liberty is gone. Change or modify the character of the element and you limit or destroy the freedom of the creature's life.[8]

So a being is most free when it is in the environment for which it was designed.

What is it like to have this kind of freedom? There is a wonderful scene in *The Once and Future King*, T. H. White's retelling of the King Arthur myth. In the story, Arthur was called "the Wart" when he was a boy, and

7. Martensen, quoted in Hopkins, *Law of Liberty*, 76.
8. Hopkins, *Law of Liberty*, 76.

one day the magician Merlin turned him into a fish. White describes what it was like for the Wart to be a fish for the first time:

> The next most lovely thing was that the Wart had no weight. He was not earth-bound any more and did not have to plod along on a flat surface, pressed down by gravity and the weight of the atmosphere. He could do what men had always wanted to do, that is, fly. There is practically no difference between flying in the water and flying in the air. The best of it was that he did not have to fly in a machine, by pulling levers and sitting still, but could do it with his own body. It was like the dreams people have.[9]

When the Wart exercises his powers as a fish for the first time, he is wonderfully free and happy. He is flourishing as a fish, and "flying" the way he has always wanted.

But what happens if such a creature is maimed? A crippled fish cannot swim as it is supposed to, and a bird with a broken wing cannot fly. Therefore, such creatures are not free. They are crippled by brokenness. According to the Bible, sin breaks us in similar ways. We are not truly free because we are debilitated by sin, unable to flourish according to how God designed us. Again, Hopkins explains:

> Through sin we have lost the inner principle of life, and we have forfeited also the sphere which is its true abode. Restoration consists in both the quickening [resurrection] of the spirit, and its introduction into its appropriate environment. To be "born again" is to receive that quickening. To be "in Christ" is to be in that environment.[10]

Here Hopkins explains how sin has maimed us: Our "spirit" (or soul) is "dead" and must be resurrected. We spiritually died when we sinned, and we could no longer be close to God. Sin maimed our souls and got in the way. But Scripture says that Jesus spiritually resurrects us when we are "born again," that is, when we first trust in his death and resurrection to pay the penalty for our sins. We are "born again," that is, reborn spiritually, in that instant (see John 3:3–17). Our souls are now free from the power of sin.

---

9. White, *Once and Future King*, 43.
10. Hopkins, *Law of Liberty*, 76.

Then, the Bible says we are placed "in Christ." In over sixty verses, the New Testament says we are "in Christ" or "in him."[11] This is our new, spiritual environment that enables us to fly. When we are placed "in Christ," we have all of his power, freedom from sin, love, joy, and peace available to us. But we *experience* his love and power when we are surrendered to Christ, "in him who is the true sphere of life."[12] Resting and surrendered in his presence and power, we are truly free. To be truly free in him is to be filled with his Spirit.

THE SPIRIT-FILLED LIFE

What does it mean to be filled with the Spirit? Gal 5:23 says, "The fruit of the Spirit is love, joy, peace, patience, kindness, goodness, faithfulness, gentleness, and self-control." The word "fruit," in the Greek, here, is in the singular. It is *one* fruit with all of its listed aspects: patience, peace, kindness, and so forth. The first three parts of the fruit—love, joy, and peace—are *states of mind*.[13] They are the result of full submission to Christ. When we submit to him, we experience *his* love, *his* joy, and *his* peace. Literally. We taste and experience the love of God, which flows into our loving acts for others. "God is love" (1 John 4:16). He is literally overflowing with love, according to Eph 3:18–19. Then we taste and experience joy, *his joy*. God's goodness is delightful, ecstatic and bursting with flavor. We experience his joy that comes from *his goodness*. And we experience the peace of God. Since God is all-powerful and all-knowing, nothing can surprise him, and nothing is more powerful than him. So he is at *peace*. We experience that same peace, *his* peace, the "peace that transcends all understanding" (Phil 4:7). And our loving acts to others flow from that.

Out of this state of mind come the other six aspects of the fruit, which are acts, disciplines, and character traits. Patience, kindness, goodness, faithfulness, gentleness, and self-control. These are gracious characteristics. "Goodness" is likely the generosity of God. This word in the Greek is translated "generous" in Matt 20:15, in which it is juxtaposed to "envious."[14] "Kindness" is the word used to translate "good" in Pss 34:8 and 136:1.[15]

---

11. Byars, "List of in Christ," paras. 6–83.
12. Hopkins, *Law of Liberty*, 76.
13. Hopkins, *Law of Liberty*, 71–72.
14. Bruce, *Galatians*, 253–54.
15. Bruce, *Galatians*, 253.

These things flow from our experience of the love of God. They are not automatically produced by something like "feelings." They are work, they are disciplines, they are habits. But our energy for them comes from feasting on God's love.

Being filled with the Spirit is so remarkable that John Piper calls it "Christian hedonism," an enjoyment of the pleasures of God. He asserts that "God is most glorified in us when we are most satisfied in him."[16] For example, Ps 34:8 says, "Taste and see that the Lord is good." Christian hedonism is the "abundant life" Jesus speaks of in John 10:10: "I came that they might have life, and may have it abundantly" (NET). The abundant life is a life of feasting on the goodness of God, which results in the power of God, the presence of God, and the holiness of God being manifested in a person's life. It is a life of true freedom: freedom from sin and freedom to obey God, freedom to experience all of God's delicious goodness, freedom to delight in *his* joy, and freedom to flourish as God designed us to flourish. It is a "happy," "blessed" life of flying as he created us to fly. How do we experience this kind of life?[17]

When we become Christians, the Spirit comes to live in us permanently, and we are in him (John 3:1–8, 14:16–17, Rom 8:9–11, 8:15–17, and Eph 1:13–14). The Spirit, as the third person of the Trinity, makes all of his resources available to us. But we only experience his love, peace, and power when we are *surrendered* to him. To surrender means to "wave the white flag," to say to God, "You can have my life, all of it, however you like." This is first done when a person becomes a Christian, but must be a constant way of life afterwards. There are many *surrenders* in a Christian's life.

How does surrender unlock the Spirit-filled life? When I sit in my car, I have access to all its power to move me from one place to the next. But if I don't turn on the ignition and press the gas pedal by faith, trusting that it will start and turn the axles to move me to my destination, I do not experience the power of the car. When we become Christians, we are placed in the car. But the car does not move unless we surrender ourselves to Christ, for him to graciously direct us. When we surrender to him, this turns on the ignition and moves the car by faith. Notice that it is the *car* that carries me. I can, of course, put the car in neutral and push it with my own strength, but

---

16. Piper, *When I Don't Desire God*, 19.

17. For introductions to the Spirit-filled life, see Bright, *Secret*; and Stanley, *Wonderful Spirit-Filled Life*. For scholarly treatments see Barabas, *So Great Salvation*; and Dunn, *Jesus and the Spirit*.

that negates the purpose of the car. The car is supposed to carry me in its own power. When I am surrendered to Christ, *his* love and *his* power carry me in order to live the holy, joyful life he has created me to live. This is what it means to be filled with the Spirit.[18] To try and live a holy, righteous life in my own power is like trying to push the car. I can push it, but I cannot get to the destinations God has in store for me. What is the point of having the car if I have to push it?

We experience the Christian life, the Spirit-filled life, by faith. Gal 2:20 says, "I have been crucified with Christ and I no longer live, *but Christ lives in me*. The life I live in the body, I live *by faith* in the son of God, who loved me and gave himself for me" (emphasis mine). Notice that I have died with Christ. My old life of sin, my old way of life, died with Christ, and now I am new in him because I have been resurrected in him. Paul describes what this means in Rom 6–8. My soul has now come alive in Christ. I have a new life now, created to be holy, and I am to live my life, "in the body," by faith. I am a new person in Christ, and I am to trust that I have that new life, that new nature in him. To live by faith is to surrender to God, to turn on the ignition and push the gas pedal, believing God's power will move me to his will and his righteous life. It is the true freedom of being carried by the car that is moving me the way it is supposed to. I was created to be in the car, to be "in him." When the car moves me, it takes me to new and exciting destinations in Christ. The more surrendered I am to him, the more fully *human* I am. I am more human because I was designed to rely on him and his joyful, holy life. When I am un-surrendered to him and living my own life, I am less human, because I am maimed and crippled by sin, unable to be who he created me to be.

The slavery of Landru in "Return of the Archons" is thus a rather harsh stereotype of the real freedom we have to fly in Christ. Since we were designed to be in Christ, we are most free when we are flourishing in him.

Importantly, this life in Christ is not a vacuous mental life. It is an exciting life of intellectual discovery, as we learn what God, the smartest being in the universe, already knows. This amazing intellectual journey begins when we become Christians and continues in heaven, where it will go on forever. It is in bowing to the overflowing joy and goodness of God that we become truly free and reach all our human potential.

---

18. See Barabas, *So Great Salvation*, 79–80, 114.

RELIGION AS THE OPIATE OF THE MASSES?

THE SPIRITUAL LIFE AND CREATIVITY

> KIRK: Without freedom of choice, there is no creativity. Without creativity, there is no life. The Body dies. The fault is yours . . . The evil must be destroyed . . . And you are the evil.

"Without freedom of choice, there is no creativity." This is, of course, true and fits with a Christian worldview. God upheld the freedom to choose between good and evil for Adam and Eve in the garden of Eden, and as we will see in volume 2, the work Adam and Eve were to do in the garden included creativity. Additionally, in chapter 11 we saw that creativity is part of heaven. It is no less a part of the Spirit-filled life, which is really a deposit of heaven in this life (see Eph 1:13–14 and John 17:3). Surrendered to God, we are more creative and more richly expressive than we could ever be without him. He is the source of all creativity, since he richly created the universe with its endless variety and beauty. Since we are made in his image, we create as he did.[19]

Several times in this episode Kirk says that because Landru is a computer, it does not have the "soul" of the original Landru who created it. The computer couldn't replicate the "wisdom, the compassion, the understanding" of the original Landru. It might seem that this leaves open the possibility that a wise, compassionate human *could* create a good, healthy paradise. But this is hardly likely. In *Star Trek*, humans are not meant for paradise, period.

> KIRK: How's it going?
>
> LINDSTROM: Couldn't be better. Already this morning, we've had half a dozen domestic quarrels and two genuine knock-down drag-outs. It may not be paradise, but it's certainly human.
>
> KIRK: Sounds most promising. Good luck.

In this scene, Lt. Lindstrom stays behind on the planet to help the inhabitants create a new society without the control of Landru. The assumption here is that imperfection is essential to being human. Conflict, even a violent nature, is *essentially* human, and therefore good. But why think this? Biblically, Adam and Eve were sinless in the garden, meaning that they did not have violent conflict, or presumably, much conflict at all. There was work and sex in the garden (before the fall), all that was necessary for Adam

---

19. Crouch, *Culture Making*, 103–7.

and Eve to flourish as human beings, and they were able to use the gifts God had given them there (again, see volume 2 on "The Apple").

Humans were created to flourish, indeed did flourish, without sin and violence. As we have seen, there truly is infinite joy in surrender to God, and flourishing creativity as we are made in his image and create as he has created. Being filled with the Spirit restores the creativity and human flourishing we lost in the garden of Eden.

Bibliography

Adams, Robert Merrihew. *A Theory of Virtue: Excellence in Being for the Good*. Oxford: Oxford University Press, 2006

Alcorn, Randy. *Heaven*. Carol Stream, IL: Tyndale House, 2004.

Alexander, David. "Gene Roddenberry: Writer, Producer, Philosopher, Humanist." *The Humanist* 51.2 (1991) 5–30, 38.

———. *Star Trek Creator: The Authorized Biography of Gene Roddenberry*. New York: Roc, 1994.

Allen, David L. "Substitutionary Atonement and Cultic Terminology in Isaiah 53." In *The Gospel According to Isaiah 53*, edited by Darrell L. Bock et al., 171–89. Grand Rapids: Kregel, 2012.

Andrews, Travis M., and Roxanne Roberts. "The Love Affair Between Jeff Bezos and 'Star Trek.'" *Washington Post*, Oct. 13, 2021. https://www.washingtonpost.com/arts-entertainment/2021/10/13/jeff-bezos-star-trek-william-shatner/.

Arenas, Jorge. "Star Trek Boss Alex Kurtzman Explains What the Mission of the Franchise Is." Bounding into Comics, Aug. 26, 2020. https://boundingintocomics.com/2020/08/26/star-trek-boss-alex-kurtzman-explains-what-the-mission-of-the-franchise-is/.

Asa, Robert. "Classic *Star Trek* and the Death of God." In *Star Trek and Sacred Ground*, edited by Jennifer E. Porter and Darcee L. McLaren, 33–59. Albany: State University of New York Press, 1999.

Associated Press. "Star Trek IV: The Voyage Home' Spotlights Greenpeace Efforts." Mar. 28, 1987.

Augustine of Hippo. *The City of God*. Reprint, London: Penguin Classics, 2004.

———. "Our Heart Is Restless Until It Rests in You—Augustine." Crossroads Initiative, July 21, 2021. https://www.crossroadsinitiative.com/media/articles/ourheartisrestlessuntilitrestsinyou/.

Barabas, Steven. *So Great Salvation: The History and Message of the Keswick Convention*. 1952. Reprint, Eugene, OR: Wipf & Stock, 2005.

Bárcenas, Alejandro, and Steve Bein. "'Make It So': Kant, Confucius, and the Prime Directive." In *The Ultimate Star Trek and Philosophy*, edited by Kevin S. Decker and Jason T. Eberl, 36–46. Hoboken, NJ: Wiley, 2016.

Batchelder, Robert C. *The Irreversible Decision: 1939–1950*. Boston: Houghton Mifflin, 1962.

Beale, G. K. *The Book of Revelation*. New International Greek Testament Commentary. Grand Rapids: Eerdmans, 1999.

Bibliography

Bernier, Mark. *The Task of Hope in Kierkegaard*. Oxford: Oxford University Press, 2015.

Bible Gateway. "High Place." N.d. https://www.biblegateway.com/resources/encyclopedia-of-the-bible/High-Place.

Blish, James. *Star Trek: The Classic Episodes*. New York: Del Rey, 2016.

Bloom, Mike. "'Star Trek' Showrunner: 'Discovery' Season 2 Is About Spock's 'Unwritten Chapter.'" *Hollywood Reporter*, Jan. 17, 2019. https://www.hollywoodreporter.com/tv/tv-news/star-trek-discovery-season-2-premiere-explained-alex-kurtzman-spocks-unwritten-chapter-1176116/.

Bock, Darrell L. *The Missing Gospels*. Nashville: Thomas Nelson, 2006.

Bright, Bill. *The Secret: How to Live with Purpose and Power*. San Bernardino, CA: Here's Life, 1989.

Brown, Michael L. "Jewish Interpretations of Isaiah 53." In *The Gospel According to Isaiah 53*, edited by Darrell Bock et al., 61–83. Grand Rapids: Eerdmans, 2012.

Bruce, F. F. *The Epistle to the Galatians*. New International Greek Testament Commentary. Grand Rapids: Eerdmans, 1982.

Byars, Clint. "List of in Christ, in Him Scriptures to Establish Your Heart in Your New Creation Identity in Christ." *Forward Ministries* (blog), Jan. 2, 2018. https://www.clintbyars.com/blog/2018/1/2/list-of-in-christ-in-him-scriptures.

Carson, D. A. *The Gospel According to John*. Pelican New Testament Commentaries. Grand Rapids: Eerdmans, 1991.

Clarke, Arthur C. "Clarke's Third Law on UFOs." *Science* 159 (1968) 255. https://www.science.org/doi/10.1126/science.159.3812.255.c.

———. "How Arthur C. Clarke Saved *Star Trek*." Arthur C. Clarke Official Website, Jan. 10, 2018. http://arthurcclarke.org/site/how-arthur-c-clarke-helped-save-star-trek/.

———. *Profiles of the Future: An Inquiry into the Limits of the Possible*. New York: Holt, Rinehart and Winston, 1984.

Colavito, Jason. "Charioteer of the Gods: H. P. Lovecraft and the Invention of Ancient Astronauts." *Skeptic* 10.4 (2004) 36–38. https://www.skeptic.com/eskeptic/04-04-26/.

Cox, Samuel J. "H-0507-1: Operations Downfall and Ketsugo—November 1945." Naval History and Heritage Command, Jan. 2021. https://www.history.navy.mil/about-us/leadership/director/directors-corner/h-grams/h-gram-057/h-057-1.html.

Craig, William Lane. *Assessing the New Testament Evidence for the Historicity of the Resurrection of Jesus*. Lewiston, NY: Edwin Mellen, 1989.

———. "Classical Apologetics." In *Five Views on Apologetics*, edited by Steven B. Cowan, 25–55. Grand Rapids: Zondervan, 2000.

———. "Men Moved by the Holy Spirit Spoke from God: A Middle Knowledge Perspective on Biblical Inspiration." *Philosophia Christi* series 2, 1.1 (1999) 45–82.

———. *The Only Wise God*. 1987. Reprint, Eugene, OR: Wipf & Stock, 2000.

———. *Reasonable Faith*. 3rd ed. Wheaton, IL: Crossway, 2008.

———. *Time and Eternity*. Wheaton, IL: Crossway, 2001.

Craig, William Lane, and J. P. Moreland. *Philosophical Foundations for a Christian Worldview*. 2nd ed. Downers Grove, IL: InterVarsity, 2017.

Craigie, Peter C. *Psalm 1–50*. 2nd ed. Word Biblical Commentary 19. Nashville: Thomas Nelson, 2004. Electronic ed.

Crouch, Andy. *Culture Making: Recovering Our Creative Calling*. Downers Grove, IL: InterVarsity, 2008.

Bibliography

Cushman, Marc. *These Are the Voyages: Gene Roddenberry and Star Trek in the 1970s Volume 2 [1975–1977]*. Los Angeles: Jacobs/Brown, 2020.
———. *These Are the Voyages: TOS Season One*. Los Angeles: Jacobs/Brown, 2013.
———. *These Are the Voyages: TOS Season Two*. Los Angeles: Jacobs/Brown, 2014.
———. *These Are the Voyages: TOS Season Three*. Los Angeles: Jacobs/Brown, 2014.
Davis, Stephen T., et al. *The Trinity*. Oxford: Oxford University Press, 1999.
DeCosse, David. "Totaling Up; It Was an Unjust War." Markkula Center for Applied Ethics at Santa Clara University, May 16, 2008. https://www.scu.edu/ethics/focus-areas/more-focus-areas/resources/totaling-up-it-was-an-unjust-war/.
Dunn, James D. G. *Jesus and the Spirit*. Philadelphia: Westminster, 1975.
Ecklund, Elaine Howard. *Science vs. Religion: What Scientists Really Think*. Oxford: Oxford University Press, 2010.
Editors of Encyclopedia Britannica. "Christian X: King of Denmark." Britannica.com, last updated September 22, 2024. https://www.britannica.com/biography/Christian-X.
Edwards, Jonathan. "A Dissertation Concerning the Nature of True Virtue." Chapter 2 of *The Works of Jonathan Edwards, Volume One*. Grand Rapids: Christian Classics Ethereal Library, 2010. https://ccel.org/ccel/edwards/works1/works1.v.ii.html.
Enemark, Christian, and Christopher Michaelsen. "Just War Doctrine and the Invasion of Iraq." *Australian Journal of Politics and History* 51 (2005) 545–63. https://papers.ssrn.com/sol3/papers.cfm?abstract_id=1673769.
Epstein, Stephen M. "Scholars Will Call It Nonsense: The Structure of Erich von Däniken's Argument." *Expedition Magazine* 29.2 (1987) 12–18. http://www.penn.museum/sites/expedition/?p=14613.
Evans, Craig A. *Fabricating Jesus*. Downers Grove, IL: InterVarsity, 2006.
———. "Messianism." In *Dictionary of New Testament Background*, edited by Craig A. Evans and Stanley E. Porter, 698–707. Downers Grove, IL: InterVarsity, 2000.
Falcon, Andrea. "Aristotle on Causality." *Stanford Encyclopedia of Philosophy*, last updated March 7, 2023. https://plato.stanford.edu/entries/aristotle-causality/#FourCaus.
Ferguson, LaToya. "Groundbreaking TV Shows That Helped Society Evolve." Yard Barker, Apr. 6, 2020. https://www.yardbarker.com/entertainment/articles/groundbreaking_tv_shows_that_helped_society_evolve/s1__31717436.
Fern, Yvonne. *Gene Roddenberry: The Last Conversation*. Berkeley: University of California Press, 1994.
Flatow, Ira, and Erin Macdonald. "Star Trek's Science Advisor Reveals the Real Astrophysics on Screen." Science Friday, May 12, 2023. https://www.sciencefriday.com/segments/star-trek-series-science-consultant-astrophysics/.
Flynn, Tom. "Secular Humanism Defined." *Free Inquiry*, n.d. https://secularhumanism.org/what-is-secular-humanism/secular-humanism-defined/.
Fortman, E. J. *Everlasting Life After Death*. Staten Island, NY: Alba House, 1976.
Galileo Galilei. *Dialogue Concerning the Two Chief World Systems*. Translated by Stillman Drake. New York: Modern Library, 2001.
Greenberg, Mike. "The Elysian Fields: The Paradise of the Greek Afterlife." Mythology Source, June 16, 2020. https://mythologysource.com/elysian-fields/.
Gregerson, Erik. "Conservation of Linear Momentum." Encyclopedia Britannica online, last updated May 16, 2024. https://www.britannica.com/science/conservation-of-linear-momentum.
Gregory, Chris. *Star Trek: Parallel Narratives*. New York: St. Martin's, 2000.
Grudem, Wayne. *Systematic Theology*. Grand Rapids: Zondervan, 1994.

Bibliography

Hagner, Donald A. *Matthew 1–13*. Word Biblical Commentary 33A. Dallas: Word, 1993.

Hannam, James. "Frequently Asked Questions on the Inquisition." *James Hannam* (blog), 2007. https://jameshannam.com/inquisition.htm.

———. *The Genesis of Science: How the Christian Middle Ages Launched the Scientific Revolution*. Washington, DC: Regnery, 2011.

———. "The Myth of the Flat Earth." *James Hannam* (blog), 2007. https://jameshannam.com/flatearth.htm.

———. "The Mythical Conflict Between Science and Religion." *James Hannam* (blog), 2009. https://jameshannam.com/conflict.htm.

———. "Science and Church in the Middle Ages." *James Hannam* (blog), 2009. https://jameshannam.com/ medievalscience.htm.

Harrison, R. K. *Introduction to the Old Testament*. Grand Rapids: Eerdmans, 1969.

Hartley, J. E. "Atonement, Day of." In *Dictionary of the Old Testament: Pentateuch*, edited by T. Desmond Alexander and David W. Baker, 54–61. Downers Grove, IL: InterVarsity, 2003.

Hauerwas, Stanley. "Pacifism: Some Philosophical Considerations." *Faith and Philosophy* 2 (1985) 277–83. https://place.asburyseminary.edu/cgi/viewcontent.cgi?article=1052&context=faithandphilosophy.

Hoehner, Harold W. *Ephesians: An Exegetical Commentary*. Grand Rapids: Baker Academic, 2002.

Hopkins, Evan H. *The Law of Liberty in the Spiritual Life*. 1905. Reprint, Fort Washington, PA: Christian Literature Crusade, 1991.

Jenkins, Henry. "What 'Black Panther' Can Teach Us About the Civic Imagination." *Global-e* 11.27 (2018). https://globalejournal.org/global-e/may-2018/what-black-panther-can-teach-us-about-civic-imagination.

Johnson, David Kyle. *Inception and Philosophy*. Hoboken, NJ: Wiley, 2012.

———. "The Prime Directive and Postcolonialism." Disc 3. *Sci-Phi: Science Fiction as Philosophy* DVD set. Chantilly, VA: The Teaching Company, 2018.

Johnson, James Turner. "Just War, As It Was and Is." *First Things* 149 (2005) 14–24. https://www.firstthings.com/article/2005/01/just-war-as-it-was-and-is.

Kaur, Harmeet. "Why People Are Reluctant to Call Themselves Atheists." CNN, Mar. 10, 2024. https://www.cnn.com/2024/03/10/us/atheism-beliefs-explained-cec?cid=ios_app.

Ketterer, David. *Imprisoned in a Tesseract: The Life and Work of James Blish*. Kent, OH: Kent State University Press, 1987.

Kinghorn, Kevin, and Stephen Travis. *But What About God's Wrath?* Downers Grove, IL: InterVarsity, 2019.

Klein, Christopher. "Egypt's Oldest Papyri Detail Great Pyramid Construction." History.com, last updated April 15, 2024. https://www.history.com/news/egypts-oldest-papyri-detail-great-pyramid-construction.

Komoszewski, J. Ed., et al. *Reinventing Jesus*. Grand Rapids: Kregel, 2006.

Koptak, Paul E. *Proverbs*. New International Version Application Commentary 15. Grand Rapids: Zondervan, 2003.

Kraemer, Ross S., et al. *The Religions of Star Trek*. Boulder, CO: Westview, 2001.

Kreeft, Peter. *Everything You Ever Wanted to Know About Heaven: But Never Dreamed of Asking*. San Francisco: Ignatius, 1990.

———. *Heaven: The Heart's Deepest Longing*. Expanded ed. San Francisco: Ignatius, 1989.

Kreitzer, Larry. "Suffering, Sacrifice and Redemption: Biblical Imagery in *Star Trek*." In *Star Trek and Sacred Ground*, edited by Jennifer E. Porter and Darcee L. McLaren, 139–63. Albany: State University of New York Press, 1999.

Kuperczko, Diana, et al. "Sudden Gamer Death: Non-Violent Death Cases Linked to Playing Video Games." *BMC Psychiatry* 22 (2022) 824. https://doi.org/10.1186/s12888-022-04373-5.

Lamb, David T. *The Emotions of God*. Downers Grove, IL: InterVarsity, 2022.

Lane, Tony. "The Wrath of God as an Aspect of the Love of God." In *Nothing Greater, Nothing Better: Theological Essays on the Love of God*, edited by Kevin J. Vanhoozer, 138–67. Grand Rapids: Eerdmans, 2001.

Langan, John. "The Elements of St. Augustine's Just War Theory." *Journal of Religious Ethics* 12.1 (1984) 19–30. https://www.jstor.org/stable/40014967.

Lau, Joe, and Jonathan Chan. Critical Thinking Web. https://philosophy.hku.hk/think/.

Lazar, Seth. "War." *Stanford Encyclopedia of Philosophy*, May 3, 2016. https://plato.stanford.edu/entries/war/.

Legrand, H. E., and Wayne E. Boese "Chariots of the Gods? And All That: Pseudo-History in the Classroom." *The History Teacher* 8 (1975) 365–66.

Lewis, C. S. *The Great Divorce*. 1946. Reprint, New York: HarperOne, 2001.

———. *The Last Battle*. The Chronicles of Narnia 7. New York: HarperTrophy, 1994.

———. *The Weight of Glory*. 1975. Reprint, New York: Touchstone, 1996.

Lockhart, P. R. "#WakandaTheVote: How Activists Are Using Black Panther Screenings to Register Voters." Vox, Feb. 21, 2018. https://www.vox.com/policy-and-politics/2018/2/21/17033644/black-panther-screenings-voter-registration-wakanda-the-vote.

Loffhagen, Matthew. "15 Star Trek Gadgets That Exist in Real Life." Screen Rant, July 4, 2016. https://screenrant.com/star-trek-real-life-gadgets/.

Longenecker, Richard N. *Biblical Exegesis in the Apostolic Period*. 2nd ed. Grand Rapids: Eerdmans, 1999.

Luzong, Allia. "Omnism 101: A Full Guide to the Omnist Belief." A Little Bit Human, Aug. 2, 2022. https://www.alittlebithuman.com/omnist-info-guide-to-ominism/.

Maples-Keller, Jessica L., et al. "The Use of Virtual Reality Technology in the Treatment of Anxiety and Other Psychiatric Disorders." *Harvard Review of Psychiatry* 25 (2017) 103–13. https://www.ncbi.nlm.nih.gov/pmc/articles/PMC5421394/.

Martin, Ralph P. *James*. Word Biblical Commentary 48. Dallas: Word, 1988. Electronic ed.

Mattox, John Mark. "Augustine: Political and Social Philosophy." Internet Encyclopedia of Philosophy. https://iep.utm.edu/augustine-political-and-social-philosophy/.

McDowell, Josh. *Evidence That Demands a Verdict: Volume 1*. Nashville: Thomas Nelson, 1979.

McKeown, J. "Land, Fertility, Famine." In *Dictionary of the Old Testament Pentateuch*, edited by T. Desmond Alexander and David W. Baker, 487–91. Downers Grove, IL: InterVarsity, 2003.

Memory Alpha Wiki. "Gene Roddenberry." Last updated October 6, 2022. https://memory-alpha.fandom.com/wiki/Gene_Roddenberry.

———. "Modern Marvels: Star Trek Tech." Last updated January 1, 2018. https://memory-alpha.fandom.com/wiki/Modern_Marvels:_Star_Trek_Tech.

———. "Trekkie." Last updated June 15, 2023. https://memory-alpha.fandom.com/wiki/Trekkie.

Bibliography

Mikkelson, David. "The King of Denmark Wore a Yellow Star." Snopes, July 4, 2000. https://www.snopes.com/fact-check/a-star-is-borne/.

Molina, Luis de. *On Divine Foreknowledge*. Translated by Alfred J. Freddoso. Ithaca, NY: Cornell University Press, 1988.

Moo, Douglas. *Romans*. New International Commentary on the New Testament 7. Grand Rapids: Eerdmans, 1996.

Moore, Frazier. "America's Most Wanted Notches 1000th Arrest." *Toronto Star*, May 13, 2008. https://www.thestar.com/entertainment/americas-most-wanted-notches-1-000th-arrest/article_451e9c33-4ef4-533c-8914-d02731170c8c.html.

Moreland, J. P. *Love Your God with All Your Mind: The Role of Reason in the Life of the Soul*. Colorado Springs: NavPress, 1997.

Morris, Thomas V. *The Logic of God Incarnate*. 1986. Reprint, Eugene, OR: Wipf & Stock, 2001.

Motyer, J. Alec. *The Prophecy of Isaiah: An Introduction and Commentary*. Downers Grove, IL: InterVarsity, 1993.

Mouw, Richard J. *When the Kings Come Marching In: Isaiah and the New Jerusalem*. Grand Rapids: Eerdmans, 2002.

NASA. "Star Trek and NASA: Celebrating the Connection." Aug. 19, 2021. https://www.nasa.gov/image-article/star-trek-nasa-celebrating-connection/.

Nash, Ronald H. *The Gospel and the Greeks: Did the New Testament Borrow from Pagan Thought?* 2nd ed. Phillipsburg, NJ: P&R, 2003.

Neece, Kevin C. *The Gospel According to Star Trek: The Original Crew*. Eugene, OR: Cascade, 2016.

Norman, Richard. *Ethics, Killing and War*. Cambridge: Cambridge University Press, 1995.

Numbers, Ronald L. *Galileo Goes to Jail and Other Myths About Science and Religion*. Cambridge, MA: Harvard University Press, 2009. Kindle.

O'Brien, Peter T. *The Letter to the Hebrews*. Pelican New Testament Commentaries. Grand Rapids: Eerdmans, 2010.

Ohlheiser, Abby. "How Martin Luther King, Jr. Convinced 'Star Trek's' Lt. Uhura to Stay on the Show." *Washington Post*, July 31, 2015. https://www.washingtonpost.com/news/arts-and-entertainment/wp/2015/07/31/how-martin-luther-king-jr-convinced-star-treks-uhura-to-stay-on-the-show/.

O'Quinn, Kerry. "Inside Gene Roddenberry's Head." *Starlog* 9.100 (1985) 18–20.

Oswalt, John N. *The Book of Isaiah: Chapters 1–39*. New International Commentary on the Old Testament 19. Grand Rapids: Eerdmans, 1986.

Packer, J. I. "Incarnation." In *The New Bible Dictionary*, 3rd ed., edited by I. Howard Marshall et al., 501–4. Downers Grove, IL: InterVarsity, 1996.

Pagels, Elaine. *The Gnostic Gospels*. New York: Vintage Books, 1979.

Pearson, Anne Mackenzie. "From Thwarted Gods to Reclaimed Mystery? An Overview of the Depiction of Religion in Star Trek." In *Star Trek and Sacred Ground*, edited by Jennifer E. Porter and Darcee L. McLaren, 13–32. Albany: State University of New York Press, 1999.

Piper, John. *When I Don't Desire God*. Wheaton, IL: Crossway, 2004.

ThePlanetsToday. "Sublimation and Comet Tails." https://www.theplanetstoday.com/comet_tails_and_sublimation.html.

Plantinga, Alvin. *God, Freedom, and Evil*. Grand Rapids: Eerdmans, 1977.

———. *The Nature of Necessity*. Oxford: Oxford University Press, 1974.

———. *Warranted Christian Belief*. Oxford: Oxford University Press, 2000.

BIBLIOGRAPHY

Porter, Steven L. "Swinburnian Atonement and the Doctrine of Penal Substitution." *Faith and Philosophy* 21 (2004) 228–41. https://place.asburyseminary.edu/cgi/viewcontent.cgi?article=1975&context=faithandphilosophy.

Rhodes, Richard. *The Making of the Atomic Bomb: The 25th Anniversary Edition*. New York: Simon and Schuster, 2012.

Roddenberry, Gene. "A Letter from a Network Censor." Disc 2, track 16. *Star Trek: The Motion Picture Original Motion Picture Soundtrack: 20th Anniversary Collector's Edition*. Columbia Records, 1999, 2 compact discs.

Rothman, Lily. "Intense Movies May Be Dangerous for People with Weak Hearts." *Time*, May 16, 2014. https://time.com/102839/intense-movies-may-be-dangerous-for-people-with-weak-hearts/.

Rothwell, Jonathan. "You Are What You Watch? The Social Effects of TV." *New York Times*, July 25, 2019. https://www.nytimes.com/2019/07/25/upshot/social-effects-television.html.

Sachsman, David B., et al. *Memory and Myth: The Civil War in Fiction and Film from Uncle Tom's Cabin to Cold Mountain* West Lafayette, IN: Purdue University Press, 2007.

Shermer, Michael. "Shermer's Last Law." *Scientific American* 286.1 (2002) 33.

Silverman, David J. "Guns, Empires and Indians." Aeon, Oct. 13, 2016. https://aeon.co/essays/how-did-the-introduction-of-guns-change-native-america.

Smith, Huston. *The World's Religions*. Rev. ed. New York: HarperOne, 2009.

Southon, Mike. "A Defense of Christian Pacifism." *Constantly Reforming* (blog), Sept. 15, 2016. https://constantlyreforming.wordpress.com/a-defense-of-christian-pacifism/.

Stanley, Charles. *The Wonderful Spirit-Filled Life*. Nashville: Thomas Nelson, 1992.

Stein, Robert H. *The Synoptic Problem: An Introduction*. Grand Rapids: Baker, 1994.

Stobie, Jay. "Recap: Star Trek: Strange New Worlds 102—'Children of the Comet.'" StarTrek.com, May 13, 2022. https://www.startrek.com/news/recap-star-trek-strange-new-worlds-children-of-the-comet.

Strobel, Lee. *The Case for Christ*. Expanded ed. Grand Rapids: Zondervan, 2016.

———. *The Case for Faith*. Grand Rapids: Zondervan, 2000.

Stulac, George M. *James*. Downers Grove, IL: InterVarsity, 1993.

Swinburne, Richard. *The Christian God*. Oxford: Oxford University Press, 1994.

———. *Providence and the Problem of Evil*. Oxford: Oxford University Press, 1998.

Tallon, Philip, and Jerry Walls. "Why Not Live in the Holodeck?" In *Star Trek and Philosophy: The Wrath of Kant*, edited by Jason T. Eberl and Kevin S. Decker, 161–72. Chicago: Open Court, 2008.

Tertullian. *Against Praxeas*. New Advent. https://www.newadvent.org/fathers/0317.htm.

Thiselton, Anthony C. *The First Epistle to the Corinthians*. New International Greek Testament Commentary. Grand Rapids: Eerdmans, 2000.

TrekMovie.com Staff. "Alex Kurtzman Hopes Gene Roddenberry Would Be Proud of Star Trek's Endurance." TrekMovie.com, Apr. 22, 2020. https://trekmovie.com/2020/04/22/alex-kurtzman-hopes-gene-roddenberry-would-be-proud-of-star-treks-endurance/.

Uhlmann, Michael. "The Use and Abuse of Just-War Theory." *Claremont Review of Books* 3.3 (2003). https://claremontreviewofbooks.com/the-use-and-abuse-of-just-war-theory/.

United Nations. "Geneva Convention Relative to the Treatment of Prisoners of War 12 August 1949." https://www.un.org/en/genocideprevention/documents/atrocity-crimes/Doc.32_GC-III-EN.pdf.

Bibliography

United States Holocaust Memorial Museum. "Rescue in Denmark." Holocaust Encyclopedia, last updated September 23, 2019. https://encyclopedia.ushmm.org/content/en/article/rescue-in-denmark.

VanderKam, James, and Peter Flint. *The Meaning of the Dead Sea Scrolls*. San Francisco: HarperSanFrancisco, 2004.

VanGemeren, Willem A. *Psalms*. Expositor's Bible Commentary 5. Grand Rapids: Zondervan, 1991. Electronic ed.

Van Hise, James. *Roddenberry: The Man Who Created Star Trek*. Scotts Valley, CA: CreateSpace, 2015. Kindle.

Walzer, Michael. *Just and Unjust Wars*. 3rd ed. New York: Perseus, 2000.

Wellerstein, Alex. "Counting the Dead at Hiroshima and Nagasaki." *Bulletin of the Atomic Scientists*, Aug. 4, 2020. https://thebulletin.org/2020/08/counting-the-dead-at-hiroshima-and-nagasaki/.

White, T. H. *The Once and Future King*. New York: Putman, 1958.

Willard, Dallas. "Jesus the Logician." *Christian Scholar's Review* 28 (1999) 605–14. https://dwillard.org/articles/jesus-the-logician.

Williams, Thomas. "Anselm of Canterbury." *Stanford Encyclopedia of Philosophy*, last updated July 16, 2023. https://plato.stanford.edu/entries/anselm/.

Wong, David. "Chinese Ethics." *Stanford Encyclopedia of Philosophy*, Jan. 10, 2008. https://plato.stanford.educlar/entries/ethics-chinese/#VirEthDaoJunRen.

Wright, N. T. *The Resurrection of the Son of God*. Minneapolis: Fortress, 2003.

Yamauchi, Edwin M. *Pre-Christian Gnosticism: A Survey of the Proposed Evidences*. 2nd ed. 1983. Reprint, Eugene, OR: Wipf & Stock, 2003.

Zagzebski, Linda. "Heaven." In *The Routledge Encyclopedia of Philosophy* 4, 249–53. London: Routledge, 2008.

Index of Episodes & Films

EPISODES

The Original Series (TOS)

Apple, The, 40, 135, 138, 146–47, 154
Bread and Circuses, 22, 65, 87–100
Empath, The, 101, 103–12
I, Mudd, 138
Menagerie, The, 69
Omega Glory, The, 40
Plato's Stepchildren, 8
Private Little War, A, 40, 43
Return of the Archons, The, 11, 40, 128, 138, 144–54
This Side of Paradise, 138
Who Mourns for Adonais?, 4, 25, 51, 52–64

The Animated Series (TAS)

Bem, 22

The Next Generation (TNG)

Who Watches the Watchers, 4, 11, 25, 37–51
Symbiosis, 40
Homeward, 42

Deep Space Nine (DS9)

Reckoning, The, 54

Discovery (DIS)

Brightest Star, The (Short Trek), 25, 27–36
New Eden, 4, 23, 65, 76–86
Sound of Thunder, The, 28

Picard (PIC)

Et in Arcadia Ego, Part 2, 127

Strange New Worlds (SNW)

Children of the Comet, 23, 65, 67–75
All Those Who Wander, 4, 23, 101

FILMS

Star Trek: The Motion Picture, 18, 20
Star Trek II, 101, 113–26
Star Trek III, 101, 113–26
Star Trek IV, 10
Star Trek Generations, 127–28, 129–43

Scripture Index

OLD TESTAMENT

Genesis

	54
1–3	115
12	35
12:1	115
12:1–3	81
15	35
15:1–2	35
15:1–6	81
18:1–15	81
22:1–19	81
48:14	32
48:17	32

Exodus

	59
20:4–6	59
24	59
33:22	32

Leviticus

5–7	108–9

Numbers

1:53	57
18:5	57

Deuteronomy

6:5	14

1 Samuel

23:6–13	71
23:11	71

2 Samuel

6:8	57

1 Kings

8:39	57

1 Chronicles

16:30	47
28:9	57

2 Chronicles

19:2	57

Ezra

7:10	15

Job

1	43
1:1	43
1:8	43

Scripture Index

Job (continued)

1:22	43
42:4	56

Psalms

16:11	131
27:4	134
34:8	150, 151
44:21	57
50:9–12	60
75:3	47
78:57–58	59
79:6	57
95	105
95:4	103, 105
102:25–27	61
103	54
103:8	55
103:13–14	55
103:19	56
104:5	47
110	13
110:1	13
136:1	150
139	32, 56
139:1–4	57
139:1–6	32
139:7–10	32
147:5	56

Proverbs

8:30–31	143
19:21	56

Song of Songs

4:7	138

Isaiah

14:24–26	70
40:28	57
53	101, 105, 107–8, 116
53:5	106
53:5–11	108
53:7	105–6
53:11	109
54:5	59
55:1–2	110
59:18	57
60:6–7	135
60:7	136
60:9	135
60:11	135
60:13	135
60:19	135
65:17	134
66:22	134

Jeremiah

42:8	57

Lamentations

3:33	33

Ezekiel

33:11	33
36:18	57

Daniel

1:4	15
1:17	15
2:20–21	70
7:27	134

Hosea

2:2	60

Zephaniah

2:2	57

NEW TESTAMENT

Matthew

1	120, 122
1:20–21	107

Scripture Index

5:31–32	90
5:38–41	90
7:7–11	36
7:15–16	30
8:26	36
10:30	57
13:44	111
13:45–46	111
16:25	147
16:27	138
17:20	35
20:15	150
21:21	34
22:41–46	13
25:14–30	34

Mark

	120, 122
3:21	123
3:31–35	123
4:40	36
9:23–24	36
9:34	84
10:45	116
11:23	34
12:30	14
13:32	119
14:60	106
14:62–65	109
15:9–15	109
15:42–46	109

Luke

	120, 122
1:26–38	107
3:14	100
4:1	14
4:14	14
6:23	138
6:31	78
10:21	14
22:19	117
24:13–32	46
24:31	135
24:34	123
24:36–42	123

John

	122
1	14
1:1	14
1:12	55
1:29	136
3:1–8	151
3:3–17	149
3:16–17	111
7:1–10	123
8:31–36	147
10:10	151
14:2	136
14:16–17	83, 151
14:20–21	83
14:26	83
15:12–13	107
16:8	83
17:3	111, 153
20:3–9	117
20:6–8	117
20:14–16	135
20:19–20	123
20:24–29	36, 46, 135
21:1–14	135

Acts

	123
1:3	46
1:24	57
7:22	15
17:2–3	83
17:13–15	30
18:4	84
18:19	84
19:8–9	84
24:12	84
24:25	84

Romans

1:18	58
1:24	58
2:1—3:20	110

Romans (continued)

3:24	110
3:24–25	109
3:25–26	110
4:4–5	110
5:6–8	55
6–8	152
8	43
8:9–11	151
8:15–17	151
8:16	83
12	93
12:1	62
12:17–21	90
13	93
13:1–4	92–93
16:17–18	30

1 Corinthians

	121, 124
3:8	138
4:5	32
6:1–3	134
11:24	117
13	33
13:12	139
15	122
15:3–8	120
15:12–15	118

2 Corinthians

11:13	30

Galatians

1:18	121
1:18—2:5	30
2:20	152
5:23	150

Ephesians

1:4–5	69
1:4–6	110
1:11	56
1:13–14	151, 153
1:18	33
3:18–19	150
5:25–32	60

Philippians

3:20–21	135
4:7	150

2 Timothy

2:12	133

Hebrews

4:13	57
9:1—10:18	110
11:19	81
12:5	84

James

	34
1:6–8	34

2 Peter

3:13	134

1 John

2:20	83
2:26–27	83
3:2	134
3:20	57
3:24	83
4:9–10	55
4:13	83
4:16	150
4:16–18	33
4:19	70
5:6–10	83

Jude

9	84

Scripture Index

Revelation

	90
4:8	137
4:10	138
5:10	134
7:9–10	137
13:8	106
19:7–9	60
20:4–6	134
21:1–2	134
21:1–3	136–37
21:4	131
21:11	137
21:16–17	137
21:18	137
21:22–23	136
21:24–25	135–36
22:12	138

DON'T MISS
Star Trek and Faith
—Volume 2—

COMING 2026

www.ingramcontent.com/pod-product-compliance
Lightning Source LLC
Chambersburg PA
CBHW050806160426
43192CB00010B/1659